Goodbye, Geraldine

Robert J. Morgan

JGC/United Publishing Corps
Rockford, Illinois
www.jgcunited.com

Goodbye, Geraldine

By Robert J. Morgan

Cover design and photo art by Rhonda Mullins Dellepiane
Susan and Bob Morgan photo on page 272 by Ken Coonley

First Edition
10　9　8　7　6　5　4　3　2　1

Published by JGC/United Publishing Corps
www.jgcunited.com

Library of Congress Card Number: 20011096169
ISBN: 0-910941-28-9

Printed in the United States of America

Dedication

I dedicate these pages to Susan, to my family, and to my friends whose love, both gentle love and tough love, nurture and sustain me.

R.J.M.

Contents

Our Sisters "Escape"

"Al grabbed a cast iron frying pan from the stove and swung hard, catching Uncle Ned on the side of the head. It made a loud, hollow, "bonggggg" that thrilled me and Tom and still rings down through the years as our own private 'liberty bell.'"

Our Sisters "Escape"

In the house at the corner of Ninth Avenue West and Fifth Street in Duluth, Minnesota, where Gram raised her own nine children and partially raised two neighbor kids before we came, and then took in our family of five when she was 63, and a few years later took in our cousins Chuckie and Lee Ann for two more years, and a couple of neighbor kids for awhile, now only my brother Tom and I lived with Gram and her son, Uncle Ned. It was 1942. The War was on and Gram was 70 years old. Uncle Ned was an indeterminate age, somewhere, around 50, we thought. I was almost ten. Tom was seven.

Gram was not quite like the Norman Rockwell version of grandmothers. She was more like a prize-fighter with a pug hairdo. Yet she was a very feminine lady with immense kindness and a sense of fair play. We all truly loved Gram. She knew it. We knew it. But she didn't take a lot of nonsense from us and had no time for psychological games. She believed in corporal punishment, sure and swift.

Gram's husband, Grandpa, ran away seven times and lived in a single room in a run-down section of downtown Duluth. He used to be a carpenter with a terrible temper and often threw hammers and saws at posts, doors, trees, and sometimes at people. Grandpa looked about 200 years old, and no one was afraid of him anymore. I delivered meals from Gram once in a while. His room, even the hallways, smelled of sauerkraut and dirty socks, so I got out of there fast. Besides I never knew what to talk about with Grandpa. All he did was curse anyway. That passed for conversation with him.

Uncle Ned is the only one of Gram's children who never left home.

At 70, Gram was the glue that held what was left together. She was caught between defending Uncle Ned's outrageous actions while keeping him in check so he didn't hurt us and making sure we stayed in school. She was always talking about how important education was even though she only went to the eighth grade.

We could never figure out why Gram was always defending Uncle Ned until the day Uncle Hank was giving us our monthly haircut and let it slip. He said Gram put Uncle Ned's eye out by accident when he was about seven. She hit him with a stick. Hank saw it happen and thought Gram still felt guilty, and that was why she let Uncle Ned get away with murder.

Our life was — is — full of unanswered questions

about family history. We finally were in on this family secret business after that because we knew one ourselves, but we promised Hank we wouldn't tell Gram.

It helped me and Tom understand why Gram was in a fix. It was guilt. That was a heavy idea for kids to understand, but we were beginning to because we were getting guilt thrown at us from the nuns and priests whose philosophy seemed to be, "If it feels good, don't do it. If it tastes good, spit it out, or you'll end up in hell."

Tom and I both figured we were going to hell anyway because we couldn't seem to live up to all the rules for getting to heaven. Our problem was that Gram backed up everything the nuns and priests said, and threw in a few sayings and poems of her own. So feeling guilty came naturally in that old house.

Even though we knew about the eye accident, it was still tough living with Uncle Ned. He pouted, pleaded to get his own way, threatened to beat us up, and went roaring out of the house about once a month intent on committing suicide. He was like a spoiled kid, only older, who outweighed us by 125 pounds, was really strong, and was sort of grotesque with a glass eye and nine fingers. He lost a finger when he was a kid, too, but no one, not even Uncle Hank, would tell us how that happened.

But just about the time we would start to feel sorry for Uncle Ned, he would do something stupid like reaching over during supper and casually switching the radio to "H. V. Kaltenborn and the News," right in the middle of "The Lone Ranger." He said it was because the war was on and he needed to hear the news of the battle front, as if H. V. Kaltenborn were the only source. And why didn't he listen to the first half of the news instead of letting us get into "The Lone Ranger?" There wasn't another working radio in the house and, if there had been, he wouldn't have let us leave the table anyway. And we were not supposed to say anything or get mad or even feel guilty for hating him when he did stuff like that.

Lu and Al, our two sisters, were living with us until they "escaped" and rented a room in the West end. Lu was 17 and Al was 16.

They ran away on a Sunday morning just as our next door neighbor Mabel and her 100-year-old mother were going to Church and pretending they weren't fascinated by what was going on. I was watching them as I was secretly rooting for Lu and Al to get away. It was sort of funny seeing all this.

Those two "hoity toity" neighbors, as we called them, were all dressed up, casually slowing down, watching the footrace, but pretending they were just walking to their car. They were listening to all the yelling, but acting as if it were a normal Sunday morning.

I figured it gave them another reason to pretend we didn't exist, as if they needed another reason.

Here were Al and Lu running out of the house, slamming doors, crying and laughing at the same time, cutting through the garden to Fifth Street with their suitcase dangling clothes, and Uncle Ned running after them, swearing. And none of them were dressed in their Sunday best.

Gram was yelling not to cut through her garden, Uncle Ned was yelling that he was going to kill them both unless they came back, which didn't make sense to me and Tom, and sure didn't make sense to Lu and Al, because they just kept running.

People running away was a problem in our family. But Lu and Al said they didn't "run away." They said they "escaped."

The night before they left, Gram heated water on the wood burning stove in the kitchen and filled the round, galvanized tub so they could take a bath in the kitchen, as all of us did. The kitchen was off limits when Lu and Al took a bath. But Uncle Ned "forgot," he said, and barged into the kitchen while Lu was bathing. She and Al both screamed and yelled at him to get out and stay out. That wasn't the first time Uncle Ned "forgot," but it turned out to be the last.

Even though they yelled, he went through the kitchen anyway and "took a good look" Lu told us later, then went upstairs to his room. Now the problem for Lu and Al was they didn't know if he'd "forget" and come back through the kitchen again. Lu was sobbing and Al tried to make her feel better. Gram, as usual, was caught in the middle, understanding how the girls felt, yet defending Uncle Ned.

When the girls were packing to leave early the next morning, Uncle Ned came downstairs and caught them. He started swearing and grabbed Lu by the arm and twisted her to the floor. Al grabbed a cast iron frying pan from the stove and swung hard, catching Uncle Ned on the side of the head. It made a loud, hollow, "bonggggg" that thrilled me and Tom and still rings down through the years as our own private "liberty bell."

Uncle Ned slumped to the floor and Lu grabbed the suitcase and ran out the door to Fifth Street with Al not far behind. Uncle Ned wasn't knocked out, just stunned, so that's when he got up and started running after them, putting on the show for Mabel and her 100-year-old mother.

Tom and I agreed on a few things about the fight. First, that was a good hit on Uncle Ned. Second, he was really tough not to get knocked out or killed. Third, although we couldn't argue Gram out of it, that Lu and Al "ran away" as our dad "ran away" and Grandpa "ran away," we agreed between us that it really was an "escape" because Uncle Ned was so furious Gram couldn't have stopped him, and who knows what would have happened?

The Entrepreneur

"We were ready to have a nice breakfast without Uncle Ned when we heard him rattling around in his room. He came down as if he hadn't been drinking at all and, without saying a word or having coffee, took his glass eye from the form-fitted eye-cup in the cupboard where he thought we couldn't reach it, washed it under the kitchen faucet, looked around to make sure no one was watching, and popped it in"

The Entrepreneur

Uncle Ned was an entrepreneur before any of us knew how to spell it. He was a self-employed roofer who wouldn't work on Saturday because it was Saturday. He didn't work from November to May either because of the bad winters, or on rainy days, or when he ran out of roofing supplies, or when there were no roofing jobs, or when he was laid up from falling off someone's roof.

Uncle Ned was the family provider.

I remember especially well the start of one of his many entrepreneurial adventures. Early that morning, I was sitting on a flat rock near Gram's flower garden. It was the perfect daydream spot, and I would go to it often on early summer mornings. The sun would come up and heat the rock. I could sit there in the cool air and think. My mind drifted between thoughts of my Mom and of my older brother Benny who was off serving in the Army Engineers.

I could hear the foghorns on the lake, and I knew they would stop blowing soon because the sun was burning off the fog. Our watchdog, Mickey, was sitting beside me like a normal dog — at least until someone came by our sidewalk and dared step in our yard.

Uncle Ned was probably still sleeping. I was sure he came home last night, but we didn't hear him. That was unusual because his boots made loud sounds when they hit the old wooden stairs and we could usually hear him bouncing off the walls and mumbling to himself.

We never knew if he'd come into our room at the head of the stairs and just start yelling or wrecking something, so it was always good to hear him head down the hall to his own bedroom. We didn't have an overhead light in our room anymore. Last week he came home late, mumbling and bumping the walls as he came up the stairs and, instead of turning down the hall to his room, came into our room and yanked the light cord out of the ceiling. He just kept mumbling and yanked it out of the ceiling as if it were part of his nightly routine, then went to his room.

Uncle Ned had two homes, Gram's and "The Green Parrot," his favorite bar. I had hoped he would stay at the Green Parrot last night. Sometimes they let him sleep it off in a booth. If he did come home, I hoped he would stay in his bedroom. He could end a daydream by just walking past.

After a while, I went back through the shed into the kitchen. Gram was fixing some oatmeal. Tom was up. We were ready to have a nice breakfast without

Uncle Ned when we heard him rattling around in his room. He came down as if he hadn't been drinking at all and, without saying a word or having coffee, took his glass eye from the form-fitted eye-cup in the cupboard where he thought we couldn't reach it, washed it under the kitchen faucet, looked around to make sure no one was watching, and popped it in. Then he went back upstairs.

Soon he was dragging something through the hall, down the wooden stairs, thumping as he went until Gram yelled "Stop it, you're going to ruin the stairs."

He was strong and proved it by picking up the huge wooden crate he was dragging and carrying it into the dining room. We wondered how he got it in the house without any of us seeing it, especially Gram.

"What's that?" Gram asked?

"It's gonna make us rich," he said.

"Ain't another of your foolish ideas is it?"

He usually blew up when Gram made fun of him, but he just said, "You'll see."

"What in the world is that contraption?" Gram asked when the boards came off and Ned set it on the dining room table.

"It ain't no contraption, Ma." Now Ned was getting a little peevish. He handled it carefully, even dusting it with his handkerchief, as he started adjusting the angular bars and blades that made it look like a mechanical scarecrow.

"Well, if it ain't a contraption, what in the world is it?"

"It's a saw sharpening machine, Ma. Lots of people need their saws sharpened."

"Oh, My! Tell me, how have these people been getting their saws sharpened so far?"

"I don't know. All I know is there's a lot of business out there — carpenters, other people. Their saws get dull."

"This is gonna be like all the other foolishness ...."

Uncle Ned didn't answer. He just kept opening the crate.

"You were gonna repair shoes and we got a shed full of old shoes. You were gonna be an artist and the lesson books weren't even opened. You were gonna ...."

"Stop it, Ma. This is different, goddammit."

"No need to swear," she admonished.

"I'm finally trying to make something of myself. And what do you do? You make fun of me."

"You're not going to leave it there?

"Yeah, right here," he said.

"On the table?"

"Just until I get it balanced and get a few saw sharpening jobs. Then I'll move it. I need a big area like this for it."

"How're we gonna get the sugar and ketchup and stuff that's usually in the middle?" I asked.

"If you don't like it, you can live somewhere

else," Ned yelled.

We ate breakfast that morning with a saw sharpening machine as a centerpiece. And it stayed there almost three years. Uncle Ned sharpened a few saws, and Gram nagged him constantly about moving it until one day the machine disappeared.

Tom and I figured he moved it to his room and confirmed it when we snuck into his room a week later. The saw sharpener was there among all the other junk, its steel arms angled in every direction, covered with Police Gazette magazines and pictures of naked ladies. His room was messier than ours.

We didn't tell Gram about the saw or the naked ladies all over his room cause we didn't see a need to get her upset all over again. Besides, Uncle Ned didn't tell her about the plaster missing from the wall in our room or the magazines spilling all over the floor from the broken boxes. Gram couldn't get all the way up the stairs because of her arthritis. "Out of sight, out of mind," Gram always said. That was about the only one of her sayings we liked.

Our Hoity Toity Neighbor

Summer Saturdays meant picking grass for the rabbits, helping Gram feed the rabbits, chickens, and pigeons, then working in the garden while our friends were playing neighborhood baseball. Miserable jobs, but nothing to commit suicide over.

The job that made death seem preferable was flushing the upstairs toilet. Most of our friends wouldn't believe it if we told them, and neither I nor Tom was going to tell them, that's for sure. It was one family secret we wanted to keep that way.

The toilet was a throwback to a simpler time, maybe the Romans. A flush tank was mounted about five feet above the toilet and was activated by a chain that released the water. A great invention we thought, but we could never remember when it worked. During the week, we carried buckets of water upstairs to flush the toilet and on Saturdays gave it a real good flushing with the garden hose.

No one in the neighborhood knew it, except

Mabel, our hoity toity next door neighbor. And we were pretty sure she wouldn't tell anyone because she pretended we didn't exist. From her bedroom, she could look in our bathroom anytime she wanted. But her curtains were closed, night and day, winter and summer.

Our bathroom curtains, what was left of them, were never closed. It looked as though there might have been a full set of lace curtains on the bathroom window sometime in the distant past, maybe about the time the flush tank broke. Over the years, small rips had become tears, tears had become gaping holes, and now the curtains looked like something you might fix up for Halloween.

We could understand why Mabel wasn't eager to mingle with us. All she saw when she looked at our house was siding coming off, a chimney missing half the bricks, and an ugly yard to match. All she heard was Mickey's constant snarling and barking and biting mailmen or anyone else who came into the yard and the fights we had that spilled from the house into the yard and into the street.

But I'm sure that bathroom opposite her bedroom was most offensive of all.

On Saturdays, when most kids were planning parties, Tom and I flushed the upstairs toilet with a hose we pulled up from the basement through a trap door in the kitchen floor. We pulled the hose up the stairs, past the right angle landing that held the grain barrel full of chicken feed, past the top of the stairs, past the old, deep closet full of mothballs, around the hallway bend, past our bedroom, into the bathroom.

I always worked the hose connection in the basement. The connection was next to the elbow of the clay pipe that carried the house sewage to the city pipes. That wasn't bad, except the clay elbow had broken years before and Uncle Ned had replaced it with part of a truck tire inner tube. When I turned the hose on and off, my head was only inches away from the inner tube that flapped and gurgled as sewage came rushing through. It wasn't bad turning it on because I'd be clear across the basement by the time all that stuff started coming through the pipe.

Gram stood by the trap door in the kitchen and relayed instructions to Tom on the landing. Tom passed the instructions to Uncle Ned, who controlled the nozzle that pointed the water into the toilet.

Because of his key position, Uncle Ned directed the operation.

"Turn it on, goddammit," he'd shout to Tom on the landing.

"Turn it on," Tom would yell to Gram by the trapdoor in the kitchen.

"Turn it on, Bobby," Gram would yell to me.

Because Uncle Ned had to shout over the flow of water, Gram usually heard his command to Tom and said "Watch your mouth. There's no need to swear."

Whenever Tom thought Uncle Ned's voice didn't carry down to Gram, Tom would yell, "Turn it off, goddammit."

And Gram would say, "Now look what you've done, you've got the boy swearing." Then she'd quickly yell, "Turn it off, Bobby."

I'd run to the hose from the other side of the basement and shut it off as fast as I could, holding my breath all the while in case that inner tube broke.

Then I'd pull the hose and it would come snaking out of the bathroom, past the mothball closet, down the stairs, past the grain barrel, through the kitchen, through the open trapdoor, and flopping down the basement stairs. It was my job to roll it into a neat pile next to the truck tire elbow on the drain pipe.

I'm sure Mabel knew what was going on. She had to steal an occasional peek through that closed curtain once in a while. She had to see Uncle Ned with the hose poised over the toilet, had to hear him yelling, "Turn it on, goddammit," and "Turn it off, goddammit," especially on summer days when the window was open. She just had to.

The Basement

"Once, when the basement flooded, my older brother Benny got to take the galvanized tub that everyone bathed in on Saturday nights down those steep stairs and row over to the fruit cellar to get some of Gram's canned goods. I hoped I'd be big enough to do that some day."

The Basement

Beneath the floor of the house was a dark, musty place with a dirt floor, a fruit cellar at the far end with Gram's jars of rhubarb, canned rabbit, currant and rhubarb jelly and "hot stuff," a tomato sauce Gram made that killed the taste of anything you put it on, and a coal bin across from the steep steps leading to the 4'X4' trap door in the kitchen.

No one ever fell down those steps, even though the trap door was open at all hours and was cut in the floor in the busiest part of the kitchen near the sink in front of Grams cupboard. It was the cupboard that held all the dishes and Uncle Ned's glass eye in a strange looking glass holder that might have been mistaken for a finger bowl if we were a finger bowl family.

We also got into the basement from the outside, where the slanted doors had to be pulled upward so we could go down four wooden steps. That door was near the coal bin where I often sat on pieces of coal and stared at the blackness until I could see spots in front of my eyes. I'd feel peaceful there, the way I felt on the flat rock outside, but instead of fresh air I'd smell the coal dust and try to blink the spots away.

Once, when the basement flooded, my older brother Benny got to take the galvanized tub that everyone bathed in on Saturday nights down those steep stairs and row over to the fruit cellar to get some of Gram's canned goods. I always hoped I'd be big enough to do that some day.

Flushing the toilet with a hose on Saturday mornings, feeding rabbits, chickens, and pigeons, killing rats with a 22 rifle during the day, then bathing in the kitchen in a galvanized tub on Saturday nights weren't the greatest ways to spend a weekend.

So, I had to be creative when the kids at school would say, "What'ja do on the weekend?" I'd make things up, like, "We went to Pike Lake canoeing and fishing and caught a lot of fish."

It was the kind of lie I never told the priest about when I went to confession. I figured it was just one of those things I had to do so I wouldn't get so embarrassed I'd have to kill myself.

Chicken Coop

"So we had roosters that didn't crow, a dog that didn't bark, rats that stayed within the confines of the chicken coop, pigeons that didn't stray, natural fertilizers that didn't stink, and a chopping block that was hidden most of the week."

Chicken Coop

The neighbors put up with us. They complained, but they put up with us.

Our Chicken coop, with imitation brick siding to match our house, may as well have been an Egyptian Pyramid because no one else for miles around had a chicken coop.

Signorellis next door had grape vines, a neat, mowed yard, and a small garden that we were always sure would one day make the cover of Better Homes and Gardens.

Across the street, the Baldinis not only kept their yard mowed neatly, but kept the vacant lot next door just as neat. Perfect for our neighborhood baseball and football games.

Across Fifth Street, Jack Adamski's house got a coat of paint every year whether it needed it or not.

No other neighbors had chickens, rabbits, pigeons, rats, and mice. No one had a dog like Mickey that killed rats and mice in the chicken coop and bit anyone who dared to step into our yard. But Mickey did not disturb the neighbors with constant barking.

No one in the neighborhood had an Uncle Ned cutting off the heads of chickens, with some of them running headless for several yards before they died. No one had an Uncle Ned who usually chose to cut off the chickens' heads on Sunday mornings when people in the neighborhood were going to Mass at St. Peter's.

And no one had a chopping block covered with blood like the one that Uncle Ned used for his grisly task. To his credit, he kept it hidden between Signorellis' grape vines and the chicken coop — except for those Sunday mornings.

The chicken coop didn't smell up the neighborhood, although the back end, where the chickens lived, had layers and layers of straw and chicken droppings which made great fertilizer for our large garden.

The front of the chicken coop was filled with rabbit hutches. The rabbits also made the chopping block occasionally. The chicken coop attic or upper floor was where the pigeons lived and was where we stored extra bales of hay and straw.

Our roosters, taking a page from Mickey, didn't crow and make noise to disturb the neighbors. They just attacked you as you came in to feed them. They kept the back end free of rats, who preferred the rabbits and pigeons anyway. We never saw a rooster attack a rat, but figured it must have happened. Why else would the rats spare the chickens?

Neither Mickey nor we could get rid of all the rats. I used the 22 rifle to pick off a few now and then, but Mickey was the rat exterminator. Tom was younger and had to settle for the BB gun to get the mice. Mickey would attack a rat, break its back, then shake it ferociously to make sure it was dead.

It was exciting to watch a cornered rat snarl and hiss as Mickey darted back and forth until he got the rat in his teeth without getting bit himself. A few rats did bite him on the nose, but that only extended their lives for a very few seconds.

So we had roosters that didn't crow, a dog that didn't bark, rats that stayed within the confines of the chicken coop, pigeons that didn't stray, natural fertilizers that didn't stink, and a chopping block that was hidden most of the week. It was a fairly peaceful scene — except for Uncle Ned chopping off chickens' heads on Sunday mornings.

What Really Happened?

There were secrets in our family. I guess there are in all families. But it wasn't the secrets that seemed strange. It was as the way doors were slammed on questions, as if the doors were thick, leaded plates that nothing could penetrate.

Locked trunks grew in our house, and Gram had all the keys. Answers were locked in those trunks, we were sure of it.

"Did Uncle Ned ever get married?" I asked.

"Hush, that's just none of your business," Gram answered.

"Did my dad ever do anything worthwhile at all?"

"Your dad left. Doesn't that say enough?"

"Someone told me Aunt May was a nun once."

"Don't ever bring that up," Gram answered, losing patience.

"Well, was she?"

"Shush, or you'll get this dishrag across the face."

Inquiry was stomped out with wet dishrags or just

plain ignored. It didn't seem to bother any of the grownups that there was no family history — or if there was, no one talked about it.

Family history on my mother's side stopped with Gram. Grandpa was living in that smelly flat downtown, but I didn't want to pursue his history any further, afraid of what I might find. All we knew about Gram was she was born in Wausau, Wisconsin, and was older than Duluth. Gram was born in 1872. Duluth was incorporated in 1887.

I knew nothing of our Dad, except he came from Seattle. Oh, and he ran away. What was there to say beyond that?

No one would tell us, so Tom and I would do our own digging. We'd sneak into Uncle Ned's room on those rare occasions when he'd leave and forget to lock his room, and we'd read old newspapers and letters. Naturally, we'd get sidetracked looking at all the dirty pictures and magazines he had all over his room. But our main purpose was to find out more about our Mom and Dad. What really happened? We were careful to put everything back in place because there was no telling what he'd do if he ever found out we were in there. Once he almost did. We heard his boots on the wooden stairs and got out in time to sneak into the bathroom and close the door. We couldn't even make it to our room, that's what a close call it was.

Or we'd go into the deep hall closet that had no

light but lots of mothballs. We found a musket rifle and an old cylinder record Victrola that had to be wound with a small crank. And a soldiers' uniform from the first World War. And a cat-o'-nine-tails whip.

Once we were able to get into the attic, which was loaded with old magazines and books and letters, but we almost fell through the ceiling. Gram would have killed us for snooping, so we didn't go back up there. But we did find old letters and documents and hid them under our bed.

That's how we found a marriage license made out to our Mom and someone named Onnie Dickley. It was before Mom met our Dad. Tom and I thought about it and somehow figured we almost didn't happen. Or if we would have been born anyway, we'd look different and have kids teasing us about our last name. Dickley. Tommy and Bobby Dickley. We'd be in fights about it every day. But everyone said he treated Mom well.

Later we found a picture of the two of them sitting on the wooden sidewalk in front of our house. Onnie was putting a flower in Mom's hair and she was holding his arm. He had on a shirt and tie and looked pretty spiffy. In every picture of our Dad, his shirt was open at the collar and looked wrinkled, as though he had slept in it or just had a fight.

In that picture with Onnie, Mom looked beautiful, as always, and happy. More than that, she looked "contented," a word we used to see on Carnation condensed milk cans when we were kids. At the top of every can it said, "Milk from contented cows." A pretty silly thing to say on a milk can, we thought.

Gram used to use that word a lot. "Be content," she'd say, or she'd ask us, "Aren't you ever going to be content?" We really didn't get the point in those days.

It's a big word in my life now, so it's a word I throw around to my kids. "Be content," I say, without bothering to explain it.

It would have been nice for Mom to be "content" more often after she married Dad, but everyone says she had a tough life with his drinking and beating her up, and not coming home with the paycheck lots of times.

Tom and I never found out what happened between Mom and Onnie, except we learned that he went into the service.

I couldn't tell Gram we had seen the marriage license or she'd have known we were snooping around, so I told her I heard a rumor about it from someone in the family. She'd figure it was Uncle Hank and he'd be able to handle that. I knew Gram wouldn't lie, so she'd at least admit Mom almost married Onnie Dickley, but she wouldn't tell us any more about it.

"Why haven't you told us about this before, Gram?" I asked.

"It didn't pertain to you kids, that's why."

"It didn't? I almost wasn't ..." and I never finished because Gram caught me with a wet dishrag.

Years later, my older brother Benny gave us lots of black and white photos, most of which I had never seen. And he took the time to tell me about them.

In the last few years, I put together a scrapbook of those old photos for each of my children, Kelly, Kerry and Michael. A Christmas gift of history. A short history, granted, but they all now had a longer history than I had. And it came without a wet dishrag.

A Black And White Photograph

One of the black and white photographs Benny gave me shows our mother holding him as a baby. She has a small bit of hair falling over her forehead and her eyes are turned up, as if she's wondering when the picture will be snapped, or wondering if she has to smile.

A crack in the black and white photograph extends across the lower half of the picture and cuts across her hand holding the rattle and my older brother, Benny.

Benny doesn't look like much, just a little kid staring off into some distant "little kid" horizon.

But Mom, boy, she's absolutely beautiful. I suppose everyone thinks their mother is beautiful, but Mom really was a stunningly beautiful lady, looking into tomorrow with that wistful look. It's my favorite picture of her.

There were five of us when Mom died at 35. My brother Tom was three months old, born with a crippled left arm, I was three years old, my sisters Al and Lu, ten and eleven, and Benny, thirteen.

I've thought of it often, what it's like to die young, dreams just out of reach. It's got to be tough, especially if you know you're dying, and I understand from Gram that Mom knew she was dying. So did my dad, but that didn't stop him from giving her a black eye that showed on her face in the casket.

In the photo, Benny's wearing a dress, this older brother of mine, one of the toughest guys I ever met, lucky to be held by Mom, though he doesn't know it. He looks pretty bored. Maybe it's the dress, knowing he can't do a damn thing about it and afraid the picture will end up on someone's bookcase.

I look at it now with a magnifying glass and see something I never noticed before. Mom's holding a teddy bear, making it look like Benny's holding it. A dress and a teddy bear for Benny, this tough, tough brother of mine.

Mom's eyes and near-smile get to me. I wish I had known her the way Benny and my two sisters got to know her. It's silly, I guess, wishing all my life I had known my mom. I've heard stories that she was really some lady.

It would be great to look at the picture now and remember, really remember something about her, like some small incident — maybe a time when she held me and I smelled her hair, or maybe a time when she caught me stealing cookies — a memory, a real memory, not just a black and white photograph.

Well, I do have a memory, but I hesitate to write it. It was long ago, yet as clear to me as the stars in a clear sky on a country road at midnight.

I was 10 years old. It was an early summer morning, still dark. I had gone to bed the night before feeling melancholy. It was summer, and we had those small screens that expanded horizontally to fill whatever size window openings a house had. One of those screens let in the breeze that night to blow over the old metal trunk near the bed and across my face. I was only half awake. But I felt a hand touching my forehead, a warm, gentle hand, and a woman's voice saying, "Don't be afraid, Son."

I knew that it was my mother's hand and my mother's voice as surely as I have ever known anything. And the reason I knew for sure, the key to that once in a lifetime moment was in the words I heard, "Don't be afraid, Son."

See, no one had ever called me "Son" before, that I could remember. Gram didn't. Uncle Ned sure didn't.

So the memory stays, and my rational mind tries to figure out some other answer.

Maybe it was the breeze, or the blowing of the curtain across my face, or a foghorn in Lake Superior, or maybe even a cat outside. Maybe it was the "longing" I went to bed with that night.

I've thought of a million reasons why it never happened the way I remember, but none of them shake the memory of the wondrous contentment and love I felt that long-ago morning.

Now I look at that cracked photograph of my mother holding my brother in a dress with a teddy bear. And I'm glad for those eyes with that wistful look, Mom's eyes reaching across the years.

The Flat Rock

"I went past the wood burning cook stove in the kitchen and quietly opened the door to the shed. Gram didn't hear too well, but Tom and I knew she could see through steel doors, and sense us doing something wrong almost before we did it,"

The Flat Rock

I couldn't go back to sleep that morning. I wanted to hang on to the feeling of Mom, so I lay there with the breeze blowing the curtain across the metal trunk. After a while, I heard Gram moving downstairs.

I wondered if I should get up and tell her what happened. I knew I couldn't tell Tom. He'd punch me in the arm and tell me I was crazy. And for sure not Uncle Ned. I couldn't talk to him about anything and had pretty much quit trying.

Gram told us of a dream she had a few weeks earlier where her son, Chuck, had appeared to her. And it turns out he was captured by the Germans that very day. Maybe she'd understand.

I got up in the dark, slipped on my pants and shirt, carried my shoes, and walked quietly down the dark and squeaky wooden steps to the kitchen. I could see a lamp on in the dining room near the old rocker where Gram sat when she wasn't working. Sure enough, she was in the rocker with her back to me, humming "The Old Rugged

Cross." It had to be her favorite song because she sang it so much. I used to get sick of hearing it, but I didn't tell her that.

Mickey was sleeping under the dining room stove, as usual. Some watchdog. If he had seen me, he would've come after me. Mickey usually bit first and worried about who it was later.

I figured I could sneak out the back shed and get to the flat rock near the flower garden.

I went past the wood burning cook stove in the kitchen and quietly opened the door to the shed. Gram didn't hear too well, but Tom and I knew she could see through steel doors, and sense us doing something wrong almost before we did it.

As I was going to the rock, the shed door made a noise and, sure enough, Mickey came tearing out after me from under the dining room stove. I got him quieted down, but now Gram saw me.

"What are you doing up so early?" she asked.

"Oh, I ... I just couldn't sleep, so I thought I'd go outside awhile."

"You look like you've seen a ghost."

"I thought Mickey was gonna tear my leg off."

"I wish he'd go after Big Helen that way," she said.

"What do you mean?

I knew what was coming next. See, Uncle Chuck, who was just captured by the Germans, was married to Big Helen and Gram thought she was going out with other guys.

Gram also thought Big Helen was sneaking onto our front porch, opening our mailbox, which was locked, and checking on the mail to intercept government checks from Uncle Chuck. Gram didn't mention the checks belonged to Big Helen anyway, since they were still married.

"I just know she's getting in here somehow and stealing the mail," Gram said again.

I knew there was no use arguing with Gram about Big Helen, who was always nice to us whenever we saw her, so I switched subjects.

"You said something about me seeing a ghost?"

She didn't answer. I think she just couldn't get her mind off the Big Helen thing, so I said, "Gram ...." She still didn't answer.

I called her name again, louder. She turned to me.

"You said something about me seeing a ghost?"

"Yes, you look pale, different. Have you been having nightmares again?"

"No, no, no. Hey, can we talk a minute?"

See, that was one of the things I liked about Gram. She'd sit and talk to you if she wasn't busy, or reciting poems. And she would talk to you as if she were talking to an adult.

I told Gram the story about Mom appearing and she let me tell it all without interrupting. Then she said something that really surprised me, and made me feel good, too. "Believe it happened. Savor it," she said. Sometimes she would surprise me with big words like that. "Savor?" I asked. "It means to think about it, especially before you fall asleep at night. Roll it around in your head and enjoy it. It will be with you always."

She spoke as if she were quoting from the Bible. I was waiting for "till the ends of the earth," but she didn't get that dramatic, and I was glad.

She said, "Thanks for telling me." She usually didn't say "thanks" because there were so many things you were supposed to do anyway.

I felt good about Gram and about Mom, and went out the back shed, where piles of cardboard boxes filled with mismatched shoes were stacked to the ceiling on both sides of the shed. Most of the boxes were splitting open like the magazine boxes in our bedroom so that mismatched old shoes kept falling on the floor. I always had to clear a path by picking up old shoes and stuffing them back into the split boxes so I could get through.

I got past all that and went out to the flat rock where I sat for a long time. It was a place to mull over the affairs of my world. I just sat there for a long time, thinking. And now I am reminded, so many years later, that Gram was right. "It will be with you always."

Ice

"*Sunlight glinted from the ice as he slipped and skidded and cursed. He swigged on a bottle, then warmed his hands in his pockets. He even knelt and seemed to pray once. Then he tried to cut through the ice with a drill too short and a saw too dull.*"

Ice

Sister Agnita, our fifth grade teacher, told us glaciers carved the Minnesota landscape. They scoured the massive basins and retreated, leaving sand, gravel, and rock to trap centuries of rain and collect water from rivers and streams. They formed what became Lake Superior, the biggest of the five Great Lakes, 350 miles long, 160 miles wide, and 1,300 feet deep. She said its deepness made it cold, so cold it didn't return bodies, and made it freeze deep in the winter.

And she convinced us this was the "Land of Hiawatha" and we were lucky to live "By the shores of Gitchee Gumee, by the shining big sea waters."

If this were true, if the glaciers carved this land for us, if they dropped the rocks that made this city, if Hiawatha himself lived in this land, why was I so often melancholy and why did I always want to get out, just go ... anywhere ... to be someplace else?

Maybe the melancholy came from the foghorns guiding ore boats under the aerial bridge. Or the moaning whistles of freight trains loaded heavy with ore for those ships.

In summer days, in this bay of Lake Superior, where "beat the clear and sunny water, beat the shining Big Sea Water," it would have been easy for someone, intent on ending his or her life, to jump in. Many did and were never found.

Not Uncle Ned. He only threatened to jump into the lake and drown himself in the deepest part of winter, when the ice in the bay was two feet thick.

And that's the threat he made again on a cold day in January. He went upstairs, got his drill and saw, and slammed the door as he left the house. "You'll never see me again," he shouted.

Everyone knew what that meant, but nobody tried to stop him. Gram got in one, "Oh, stop your foolishness," remark but he was already out the door.

Tom and I, instead of trying to sneak into his bedroom after he left, followed him, staying far enough behind so he couldn't see or hear us, hiding behind houses and light poles along the way like junior detectives. It was almost as dangerous as risking him catching us in his bedroom, but the thought of watching him cut a hole in the thick ice and jumping in thrilled us even as it scared us. Somehow we knew he wouldn't do it, yet neither of us talked about what we'd do if he actually went through the ice.

Sunlight glinted from the ice as he slipped and

skidded and cursed. He swigged on a bottle, then warmed his hands in his pockets. He even knelt and seemed to pray once. Then he tried to cut through the ice with a drill too short and a saw too dull.

That wasn't his first failed trip to finish himself off in the ice and probably wouldn't be his last. Maybe that's why Tom and I didn't have any plans to pull him out once he went in.

He'd always return from those failed trips drunker than when he left and never say anything about it. But he'd leave the short drill and dull saw somewhere in the dining room or kitchen as reminders that he wasn't through yet.

I told Father Logan about our Uncle's threats and he assured me no one ever killed himself that way. Father sometimes spoke like Hiawatha. "Too cold. Too thick." he said.

Maybe who I was and what I became started with the glaciers, and the foghorns in the bay, and the whistles of the freight trains, and Mom dying early, and Gram's poems and sayings, and Uncle Ned, especially Uncle Ned, maybe all those things.

Maybe the glaciers and foghorns only added layers. I never thought of that in the beginning. I just wanted Tom and me to get out of there, but I knew we couldn't. Not yet, maybe not ever.

Have All The Food You Want

That evening at supper, Uncle Ned, sober now and silent about the suicide attempt, did what he often did when we were all eating together. He dipped his spoon into the sugar bowl, heaped it with sugar, then slowly moved it toward his coffee cup, only to go back, dump some back into the sugar bowl, then slowly move towards his cup again before returning to the bowl to dump more sugar. This dance of the sugar spoon went on, sometimes for a full minute, until only a few grains were left on his spoon which he put in his cup and stirred for a long time to show us how little sugar he used.

It was one of his many variants on the theme, "Don't eat too much. I'm paying for this and don't you forget it, you snot nosed kids!" He did the same thing with jelly and peanut butter, and sometimes with meat and potatoes.

So it was a defiant act when Tom, waiting until Uncle Ned was sipping his coffee, quickly took a heaping spoon of sugar and plopped it in his cocoa.

Uncle Ned slammed his cup down, raised his arm, and smashed his fist down on the table. Plates, cups and silverware jumped off the table. Only the saw sharpener stayed firm. Then somehow, in the same fluid motion, he plucked his bouncing cup of hot coffee and flung it across the room against the wall behind the stove that heated the house. The cup shattered and coffee dripped down the charred and curled wallpaper. Pieces of the smashed cup rattled to the tin floor covering that held the stove, waking Mickey, who roared out from under the stove barking and snarling at anyone and everyone.

"You Morgan's ain't gonna eat me out of house and home, goddammit!"

Tom and I knew exactly what was coming.

"Your Dad was garbage and you kids are garbage, goddammit!"

Gram was able to get in one "Watch your language" before he went on.

"No snot nosed kids are gonna throw me outta my own house."

He then bent his head slightly and popped his glass eye into his throwing hand and flung the eye across the room to shatter on the wall and mix with the smashed cup and coffee.

When Tom and I talked about it later, we thought Uncle Ned could have been a major league shortstop the way he threw the cup and glass eye in such sweeping, smooth motions. But we also wondered how he could have been so clumsy, not being able to cut through the ice that morning.

He returned to form, knocking over his chair and stomping up the staircase to his bedroom, shouting a repeat of, "You Morgan's ain't gonna drive me out of my house, goddammit."

He slammed his bedroom door and pounded spikes around the door frame once again as he nailed himself in his room.

Whenever Tom and I were able to sneak into his room, which wasn't often because he usually kept it padlocked, we'd count the holes in the door frame until it got into the hundreds. Then we gave up. With so many pictures of nude women scattered all over, we didn't have time to take a good count of nail holes.

We helped Gram clean up the coffee and glass eye mess, then we all listened to "The Lone Ranger" in it's entirety, sort of a bonus for not having him there.

Later we went upstairs to the bathroom and heard the humming of the movie projector coming from his room. We were pretty sure he was showing himself dirty movies again.

He'd show Laurel and Hardy or Tom Mix movies to all of us once in a while on his 8 millimeter home projector when he was in a generous mood. One night when Aunt May came over and the lights went out, a movie of naked men and women flashed on the screen. Uncle Ned quickly shut off the film, flipped on the lights and, red faced, stuttered an explanation, "Uh, uhh, oh, I'm sorry. I don't know how that damn movie got in there. The distributor musta sent it by mistake."

As we were finishing the meal we heard the "creeeek, ereeck" sound of spikes being pulled out of his door frame. He was on his way down again. But he wasn't stomping. He was in one of his other moods, and we didn't know which one until he came into the kitchen and said in a meek voice, "Tommy, will you help me carry my mattress down?"

That was going to be tough for Tom with his crippled left arm, but it must never have occurred to Uncle Ned.

"What in the world ...? " Gram started to ask.

"Don't worry about me," he said.

"I'm not worried about you, but what ...?"

Uncle Ned didn't let Gram finish. He turned to go back upstairs and Tom followed, looking back at me with a grin that, fortunately, Gram didn't see.

We heard footsteps as they dragged his mattress through the hall, down the stairs, and into the kitchen, Uncle Ned carrying the front and Tom struggling to carry his end, which kept flopping around, dragging on the floor half the time.

Gram was quiet as they passed through the kitchen.

"I'm gonna sleep in the Chicken Coop," Ned said.

Gram still didn't say anything.

"I'm being pushed out of my own house, but I

don't mind," he added.

This time Gram answered, "It's the most foolish thing I ever heard of. It's 30 below out there."

Uncle Ned said to Tom, "Come on, little pal. Give me a hand."

"Little Pal!" We never heard him call us anything nice before. He usually didn't even bother to call either of us by name.

Now Gram was playing it tough. She said, "If you want to be a fool, go ahead. I'm not coming after you."

Ned didn't answer as he and Tom pulled the floppy mattress through the kitchen, then the shed, hitting the stacked cardboard boxes so mismatched shoes were falling all over the place. Then they dragged it through the snow to the chicken coop.

In about five minutes Tom came in, trying not to laugh because he knew Gram would defend Uncle Ned.

"It's no laughing matter," she said.

"I ain't laughing, Gram." he said.

"You are, too. Remember, he works hard to put food on the table."

"Okay, okay," Tom said. He knew it was useless to argue.

We were helping Gram with the dishes when the shed door jerked open and Uncle Ned roared into the kitchen and shouted, "No Morgan snot nosed kids are gonna push me outta my own house, goddammit."

He was cold from the freezing weather, but fuming so his breath came out like steam. We stayed out of his way and tried not to make eye contact. Gram didn't say anything either.

That's the way it was for what seemed like ten hours. He paced from the dining room to the kitchen and would open the kitchen cupboards and look at the spot where he kept his glass eye, then slam the doors shut and pace some more, all in silence. Finally he went to his bedroom. He must have slept on the box springs or on the floor because he left his mattress in the chicken coop all night.

Tom and I dressed in heavy socks, stocking caps, and long underwear and snuck up the squeaky wooden stairs to bed. We thought it might have been easier all around if the ice in the bay hadn't been so thick.

Red Hot Coals And A Nasty Dog

"We called Mickey a "rat terrier" even though there wasn't such a breed because his favorite pastime was hunting and killing rats in the chicken coop. Cornered rats snarl and hiss and arch their backs to look bigger. None of this frightened Mickey."

Red Hot Coals And A Nasty Dog

The next night everything was quiet at supper until a red-hot coal hit Mickey's back and bounced to the floor where it cooled as it burned its way through the linoleum, already spotted with hundreds of burn holes.

Mickey shot out from under the stove again, growling, trying to bite the spot on his back where the hot coal landed. He ran into me and I tried to calm him down as I scooped up the hot coal and tossed it back on the metal stand that supported the four-legged, coal burning stove in our dining room.

Mickey slept under the stove winter and summer and had been hit with dozens of fiery coals since the grates started failing last winter. With the flying hot coals, the exposed pipe that charred and curled the wallpaper behind the stove, and the half-finished chimney, it had to be our Irish luck and a responsive fire department that kept the house from burning down.

The hot coals didn't help Mickey's temperament, already nasty to family and nastier to mailmen, moving vehicles, other dogs, and rats, especially rats.

We called Mickey a "rat terrier" even though there wasn't such a breed because his favorite pastime was hunting and killing rats in the chicken coop. Cornered rats snarl and hiss and arch their backs to look bigger. None of this frightened Mickey.

The rats killed the pigeons, chickens, and tame rabbits in the chicken coop and seemed especially vicious in the way they killed the rabbits, the meekest of the animals. More than once, we'd see a rabbit apparently feeding, and when Gram tried to shoo it away to put food in its bowl, she'd discover that a rat had eaten the rabbit's brains, nothing else.

The next morning, when we were doing the feeding, Gram and I heard scratching in the 55 gallon metal drum that held the chicken feed. It sounded like rats had gotten in, but couldn't get up the steel sides to escape.

Mickey was with us and was going crazy barking and snarling, jumping up the outside of the metal drum trying to get the rats. We knew he'd be bitten so Gram held the cover open and yelled for me to run and get the pitchfork.

I jabbed with the pitchfork as Mickey barked and snarled and chickens flapped around, clucking and running all over the place. One rooster decided it was wake-up time or maybe get-even time because it was crowing like mad. The rats were clawing and scratching up the sides of the drum trying to get out and hissing with their teeth bared when they knew they were about to get it. Meanwhile Gram was yelling over and over, "Get 'em, Bobby, get 'em."

I killed all the rats except for one that ran up the pitchfork over my bare hand and fell right at Mickey's feet. That rat didn't last long.

And Gram, boy, was she happy. She even gave me a hug while I still held the bloody pitchfork and Mickey was yipping and jumping at the sides of the steel drum trying to get more rats. Not exactly a "Norman Rockwell" scene, but it sure felt good.

Messing Up My Birthday

My ninth birthday was so special that just about the whole world remembers it — even though it was messed up.

I made sure I brought in a couple armloads of lath that day. Gram used it as kindling for starting the cook stove fire every morning. Uncle Ned had loads of lath and plaster from construction sites dumped in our yard, and it was Tom's and my job to separate the lath from the plaster and keep a pile of lath by the stove in the kitchen.

I wasn't just being industrious, I was laying the groundwork for my birthday celebration later in the day, a day of no school because I happened to be born on the Feast of the Immaculate Conception. It almost made going to a Catholic School worth it.

My ninth birthday was Dec. 8, 1941. The war had started the day before, but we didn't know about it until my birthday. Gram waved me quiet and motioned to the smaller wooden radio that worked. It sat on a larger, floor model wooden radio that never worked.

President Roosevelt said, "Yesterday, December 7th, 1941, a date which will live in infamy, the United States of America was suddenly and deliberately attacked by Naval and Air Forces of the Empire of Japan."

The Japanese had attacked Pearl Harbor. "An act of war," Roosevelt said.

It sent shivers through me, but then I thought about my birthday.

"Oh, man."

"Hush up," Gram said, her right hand, the wet dishrag wielding hand, held up to warn me.

Gram couldn't stop me from thinking about what a rotten deal this was, declaring war the day before my birthday, and announcing it on my birthday.

Tom wasn't there, Uncle Ned wasn't there, Benny was out somewhere. It wasn't until years later I realized Gram and I heard history being made. But all I could think of was, "Who wants to celebrate a kid's birthday the day after the world goes to war?"

Christmas

"The driver ran for his truck, pants leg flapping, and I tried to stop Mickey, who was no longer barking, only snarling, a bad sign for that driver. The guy made it to the truck in time, but he was still swearing like mad."

Christmas

All signs pointed to a good Christmas. Uncle Ned put up the lights on the tree without getting drunk, threatening suicide, or warning us this would be the last year he'd do it.

Gram had left the living room door open since Thanksgiving to keep it warm for Christmas. Usually it was open only a few days before and after Christmas to conserve heat. Otherwise it was like an ice box.

Uncle Ned even talked about driving Gram to Midnight Mass in his battered Diamond T truck. He wasn't going in, of course, but he said he'd drop Gram off and pick her up, something he never mentioned before that we could remember.

Gram got a letter from Benny. He was somewhere in the Pacific and said he was fine. We were all glad about that.

Oh, and one more thing. Gram said I could go to Midnight Mass by myself, even if she didn't go. I think it was because she wanted me to be an altar boy at the Midnight Mass someday. Usually we couldn't stay up past 9 o'clock in winter. That alone was a big deal. Tom was upset he couldn't go, but he was only eight and I suppose Gram had to draw the line somewhere.

Anyway, Christmas plans were humming along until Christmas Eve. We had eaten supper and Uncle Ned went upstairs. Tom and I were helping Gram clear the dishes when we heard the outer porch door bang open and someone bounce against the mailbox and inner wall, then pound on the front door like crazy. Mickey was barking and snarling, wanting to get at the intruder. Tom held Mickey. Gram told me to open the door.

It was a big, burly guy holding a basket of fruit and canned goods and looking annoyed, as if it were our fault he wasn't out getting drunk and having fist fights instead of delivering stuff on Christmas Eve.

"You Mrs. Hallfrisch?" he demanded.

"What is this?" Gram asked.

"A Christmas basket, what does it look like? Sign this and I'll be off." He pushed a delivery slip and pencil in front of Gram.

I had to go over and help hold Mickey who wanted to tear the big guy to shreds.

"We didn't order this," Gram said.

"Lady, no one orders this stuff. It's from Christian Charities. Get it?"

"No, I don't 'get it,'" Gram answered firmly, showing she wasn't going to let him push her around.

"Hey lady ... charity ... know what I mean? Now

sign this so I can get outta here."

"We don't take charity," Gram said.

"Lady, I don't care. Sign this damn thing."

He was really getting irritated and shoved the paper in Gram's face.

"Get Uncle Ned. I'll hold Mickey," I told Tom, who went rushing up the stairs.

"Give it to some poor family." Gram was calm, treating him as if she were talking to one of us.

The big guy was really exasperated now, and he pushed Gram on the shoulder as he tried to get her to sit down and sign his delivery slip.

"Hey, lady, I just do what I'm told. Now sign this damn thing and I'll get out of here."

I let Mickey go. He didn't bark, he just jumped for the guy's crotch and ripped his pants from the inside of his leg all the way down to his ankle. Then he went after his bare leg. Gram was yelling for me to get Mickey, which I was trying to do. Uncle Ned came running into the dining room and, without a word, turned the guy around, grabbed his coat and belt and pushed him out the door, through the porch, knocking the mailbox off the wall, then threw him down the four steps into a snowbank. Tom was holding Mickey now and Gram told me to take the basket and put it in the man's truck.

So, while the guy was picking himself out of the snow and yelling and shaking his fist at Uncle Ned, I carried the basket to his truck, which had the name

"Christian Charities" written on the side in big letters, so everyone in the neighborhood would know about the basket of fruit.

Meanwhile Mickey was barking and Uncle Ned was yelling, "And don't come back...goddaaaaammit!"

I closed the side door of the truck after putting the basket in, and saw Mickey tearing past Uncle Ned, going after the driver as if he were the biggest rat Mickey's ever had a chance to attack. And who was there watching the whole thing, but our hoity toity neighbor Mabel, puttering with her outdoor light display, something she always made into a big deal.

Up to then Mabel was watching everything, but acting as if nothing were going on, as if it were a quiet night before Christmas in the neighborhood. Her 100-year-old mother was watching out the front window, too, naturally. Mabel saw me, but acted as if she didn't. She just kept fooling with the lights, screwing bulbs in and out so the whole string kept going on and off.

The driver ran for his truck, pants leg flapping, and I tried to stop Mickey, who was no longer barking, only snarling, a bad sign for that driver. The guy made it to the truck in time, but he was still swearing like mad.

When the action picked up even more with the race between Mickey and the driver, Mabel wasn't even pretending to be interested in her lights anymore. She stared at me. As I took Mickey back to the house, he was barking like crazy again. Without even thinking, I said

"Merry Christmas" to Mabel. I don't know why I did it, but she acted like I had slapped her 100-year-old mother in the face, and she turned around and slammed the door.

Gram, who was calm when that big guy was trying to bully her, was upset now, not at the delivery guy, but at the person who put our name in for charity.

"Who would have done that?" she kept asking no one in particular, as though someone had just turned us in to the government for being Nazi spies.

Uncle Ned was straightening out his shirt and getting ready to go upstairs again. "Still want to go to Midnight Mass?" Ned asked Gram.

"No, I don't think so," Gram said.

"Well, then, I'm gonna hit the sack," he said.

Gram turned to me and said, "Start getting dressed. You can go to Mass, but come right home."

"Can I go?" Tom asked.

"No. Maybe next year."

"Aw, jeez Gram." Tom said.

"Watch your language and get to bed," she said, trying to act as though the big commotion hadn't upset anything.

"Big Helen," Gram said suddenly. "She's the one. Just to embarrass us."

"Gram, Big Helen's wouldn't do something like that," I argued.

"It had to be Big Helen. Get ready, now."

The argument was over.

I started walking down Ninth Avenue past Mr. and Mrs. Signorelli who were going to St. Peter's, the Italian church in the neighborhood. I turned on Fourth Street and walked the rest of the way by myself.

Midnight Mass was a bell ringing, communion taking, priest chanting, prayer singing time that made me forget everything else for a little while. Monsignor Lynch really kept things humming. Someday I wanted to be an altar boy at Midnight Mass because it was a big deal and everyone knew it.

The choir even sang "Silent Night " and a couple of other songs we could understand before Mass started.

After Mass, the nuns served hot chocolate in a schoolroom for any of the kids who wanted to join them. I stayed awhile and the nuns were laughing and joking just like real people. Even Sister Agnita. I couldn't get over it. I wondered how someone who could slap your knuckles that hard with a Coca Cola ruler could be so pleasant after Midnight Mass. Made me believe in miracles.

I watched the snow falling out the window as I was drinking my last hot chocolate, then left for home with real good feelings about everything.

Once I got a little way from church, it looked as though no one was out because there were no footprints in the snow along Fourth Street. It was snowing harder now, and my footprints were getting covered almost as fast as I made them.

I started thinking about that big guy getting thrown out of our house. What if he were just waiting out there somewhere, ready to get even by beating me up? There was no Mickey, no Uncle Ned, no Gram to keep him in line with her calm voice. Just me and my footprints.

So I decided to walk backwards up the hill, figuring it would be a little confusing, until I could get mixed in with people coming up from St. Peter's. Then I'd walk normally and, if no one was around when I got home, I'd unscrew bulbs in Mabel's big display so all the lights would go out. She wouldn't suspect me because she didn't know I existed.

Yup! It looked like it was going to be a terrific Christmas after all.

Another Christmas

The very next year brought another warm and wonderful Christmas story. Well, not so warm and wonderful really, but ... it is a story ... and it is about Christmas. It was one of those magic evenings. All the Christmas tree lights were lit and Uncle Ned wasn't. Beautiful Christmas music was playing, Midnight Mass was coming up in a couple of hours and, most important, it was time to open gifts.

I was intrigued by one of my gifts. It was shaped like a box of candy. It wasn't quite heavy enough, but what could it be?

I tore off the wrapping paper and, sure enough, it was a candy box with pictures of chocolate covered cherries on the top. I was so excited I didn't even open the box. Imagine, a "poor kid" getting a box of chocolate covered cherries all to himself! I couldn't believe it.

I leaped to my feet and ran to Gram and kissed her and hugged her and thanked her for the candies.

Even as I was hugging Gram, all I could think of

was how good the chocolate would taste and how the cherry inside each mound of chocolate would be surrounded by all those delicious juices and would pop in my mouth. Mmmmm!

No one else was going to get any either. I had already made up my mind about that, even before I finished hugging Gram. Christmas or no Christmas. A whole box. Wow!

Then I opened the box.

It was two pairs of large brown stockings. Ugly, long brown stockings. I can see them yet. My life had just ended. Eleven years old, and my life was over. Not only that, but I knew I'd feel like a sissy wearing those dumb things and I'd have to fight my way from the front door of the house all the way to school.

Dominus Vobiscum

"As we genuflected, Tom knelt on a button on his altar boy cassock and the Bible and ornate stand tumbled to the marble altar, bending one of the stand legs and sending the Bible flying off another few feet. I grabbed the stand and tried to straighten out the bent leg while Tom went after the Bible. Monsignor Lynch was not only staring at us, he was staring through us now and I could see steam rising from his head."

Dominus Vobiscum

I liked the good old days when "Dominus vobiscum" really meant something.

As an altar boy I had no idea what it meant, but I was lucky to be able to say "et cum spire tu tuo" to Monsignor Lynch, the toughest priest I ever knew. He was tougher even than Father Logan.

I never forgot any of the Latin responses. Monsignor Lynch didn't tolerate lapses of memory by his altar boys, especially not in front of the whole school, which started off every Friday morning in Church.

There was a great mystery to the Church in those days and it started with Latin. No one spoke Latin, and I was pretty sure no one knew what it meant anyway.

Then there were the rituals of the Mass. We knew what some of those meant, like the breaking of the host, which meant Christ shared the bread and wine with his disciples. I figured everyone knew that, even though it was cloaked in those Latin phrases. But it all fit. It all went with the package.

I was one of the altar boy recruits in the fifth grade. It took me a few years, but I knew if I didn't screw up too badly in serving mass, especially with Monsignor Lynch, I could one day do what I was doing that day — saying "et cum spiritu tu tuo" in front of the entire student body.

When I'd say things like that, everyone would genuflect, kneel, stand, sit, or come to the communion rail. That kind of power in the fifth grade was something really worth going for.

Of course it wasn't what I said that made all the people move around in church, it was what the priest said. I only answered him, but it seemed like the completion of a pact — from God to the priest and from him to me and then to all the people kneeling down and standing up and coming to the communion rail. It was heavy duty stuff in those days of mystery.

Monsignor Lynch was an imperious sort who didn't bother talking to altar boys except to order them around. And he didn't tolerate incompetence. I was lucky I knew my Latin answers and didn't mess up on the altar much, until that fateful Friday morning two years later. I was in the ninth grade. Tom was in the sixth.

It was Tom's big day as an altar boy, his first shot at serving Mass on Friday in front of the entire school. By now, I was routinely serving at those masses, plus serving at Midnight Mass on Christmas Eve and on Easter Sunday and even at funerals conducted by Monsignor Lynch. That was a big deal because it meant the dead person was still pretty important or Monsignor Lynch wouldn't have bothered. So I had a lot to lose.

Tom was doing beautifully until it came time to transfer the big Bible that sat on an ornate golden stand, from the right side of the altar to the left. We got up, genuflected, and Tom went to get the Bible and I crossed over to get the sacred cloth. I hadn't thought about it when I set up the sides for each of us or I would have reversed sides. The Bible was heavy and awkward and Tom's crippled left arm couldn't lift it up completely. Now it was too late.

Tom struggled to lift the stand and somehow made it, carrying it precariously from the altar down the steps to genuflect with me at the base of the altar before crossing to the other side. His fumbling caught the eye of Monsignor Lynch, and I knew there was going to be trouble. When Monsignor looked at you that way it was like he cast a spell.

As we genuflected, Tom knelt on a button on his altar boy cassock and the Bible and ornate stand tumbled to the marble altar, bending one of the stand legs and sending the Bible flying off another few feet. I grabbed the stand and tried to straighten out the bent leg while Tom went after the Bible. Monsignor Lynch was not only staring at us, he was staring through us now and I could see steam rising from his head.

I switched sides with Tom when we got the Bible and stand together and carried it to the left side of the altar with whatever dignity I had left. But it wasn't enough for Monsignor Lynch, who was flashing lightning from his eyes.

I was pretty shook up. So when I thought it was time for communion, I signaled Tom to meet me in the center so we could genuflect and get the paten, a gold-plated, saucer like dish that altar boys used to put under the chins of those taking communion. My getting up to get the paten was a clear signal to the church members who wanted communion that it was time to come to the communion rail.

But it wasn't the right time. I misread Monsignor Lynch's moves.

Even Tom knew that, but he figured I had saved him once, and I was responsible for giving him his big chance, and I'm his older brother and all that, and I must know what I'm doing, so he went along with it.

I was as good as dead now because about 20 classmates who weren't paying close attention and who also thought I knew what I was doing, came to the communion rail and knelt there. Most of them soon realized they had been sucked in by my mistake and, one by one, they dribbled back to their seats.

I guess I could have made it through that second major mistake, knowing I'd never serve mass again for Monsignor Lynch, but the real problem was Geraldine, my secret girlfriend. She just kept kneeling there at the communion rail. I liked her but hadn't got up the nerve to tell her, and maybe she liked me, too, and maybe that's why she stuck it out at the communion rail for what seemed like two hours before Monsignor Lynch was finally ready.

I think he dilly-dallied to let me suffer even more. I could almost hear him saying to himself, "I'm going to let this idiot fry in his own soup" or some such thing. He used to mix his metaphors when he really got mad.

Tom and I were banished from serving Friday Mass for two years, which was especially unfair for Tom. It was his first go at it. I had gloried in it for a couple of years until my downfall that day.

I can still hear Monsignor Lynch berating us and the "idiot" who let us serve Mass in the first place, forgetting he did it himself and that I had been one of his favorites for all those years. But it all went out the sacristy window that morning.

In those days, our lives centered on the Church and the Catholic School called "Cathedral," eight blocks from Gram's home. That life almost pulled me into wanting to be a priest someday, until I met Geraldine, but I was sure any hopes of romance with her were gone, too, after the communion disaster.

The Sacred Heart Of Jesus

Who would hang a picture about six inches from the ceiling and right next to the window frame? In the bedroom Tom and I shared, that was where someone had hung one of those religious pictures some Catholics have, a picture that shows Jesus holding what looks like a shawl to one side and showing his heart on fire.

I used that picture to help me pray sometimes. I was praying one moonlit night so my mind wouldn't wander back to Geraldine, who still wasn't talking to me. My mind wandered anyway and I wondered why anyone would hang a picture there. I decided I would ask Gram in the morning.

While my mind was drifting back and forth, I managed to say a short prayer, "Dear Jesus, please let ..." Then I think, "I can't be bothering God about something like this," but I do it anyway and pray, "Please let Geraldine talk to me again."

The moon didn't light the picture completely, so I got up to take a closer look. I made the sign of the cross in the dark because the prayer was over. I pulled the covers aside and stood on the metal packing trunk under the window by the bed. I didn't have to climb over Tom because he was sleeping on the inside near the wall. The younger brother always sleeps by the wall. It's where I used to sleep before Benny went into the Army. I stood on the trunk, reached for the picture, and hit it accidentally. It fell down, hit the metal trunk, broke the glass, and woke Tom.

"Hey, what's going on?"

"I wanted to take a closer look at that picture."

"Are you crazy or something? It's the middle of the night."

"I know, I know, don't worry about it. Go back to sleep." I was trying to whisper so we wouldn't wake up Uncle Slug. Tom and I had started calling Uncle Ned "Uncle Slug" because he was always slugging us around. Calling him that made us feel better.

Tom said in a loud voice, "Go to sleep? How can I go to sleep with you standing on the trunk knocking pictures off the wall, looking like a goon? How do I know you're not gonna hit me with a two-by-four or something?"

"Have I ever hit you with a two-by-four?"

"No, but ..."

"But nothing. Go to sleep." We were back to whispering again.

"Hey, there's a hole behind the picture. It's stuffed

with an old shirt or something."

"Lemme see." Tom got on the trunk and I had to lift him up to see the hole.

"Whatdya think?"

"I don't know. Looks 'bout the size of Slug's fist."

"Yeah, yeah, it does, doesn't it?"

"Maybe he got mad one day and poked his fist through the wall."

"Yeah, I'd love to have seen that. Been funny if he hit the window frame instead."

"Yeah, then he covers it up with a holy picture. What a rat!"

"And it's been hanging in that goofy spot for all these years."

"Yeah."

"Okay, I'll hang it back up there."

"But the glass is broken."

"So what. Gram never comes up, and Slug'll never notice."

"Yeah, go ahead," Tom said. Then he asked me, "How come you decided to check it out in the middle of the night?"

"Because I was saying a little prayer, that's why."

"Praying? What for?"

"What the hell's going on up here in the middle of the night?"

Our bedroom door slammed open and Uncle Ned's' big frame filled the opening — and there I was standing on the trunk, in the moonlight, right in front of the window.

I didn't dare say anything about it, but I wondered if he remembered all the times he woke us up when he came home drunk. Instead I said, "The picture fell down and I'm putting it back up."

"Don't lie to me. That goddammed picture didn't just fall by itself!" he shouted, moving through the moonlight so I could only see his legs, far apart now in that stance he always took before he hit us.

I didn't know what to say, but it really got to me that he was swearing about a holy picture that was helping me pray. "Who does he think he is anyway?" I said to myself.

"What in the world's going on up there in the middle of the night?"

Whew, it was Gram's voice just in the nick of time. She used that phrase again, "in the middle of the night." It was probably only about 9:30 or so. We didn't have a clock in our bedroom, so we couldn't be sure.

Gram always went to bed early, then got up and prowled around a lot, checking the outside thermometer, keeping the stove going, and sometimes just sitting in the rocking chair singing or humming "The Old Rugged Cross" or "Red River Valley" or some other sad song.

Uncle Ned would go to bed early when he wasn't out drinking, then get up and do his own prowling, sometimes opening the trap door in the kitchen and leaving it open while he roamed around in the basement. Or he'd go to the chicken coop and just sit out there with the 22 rifle and a flashlight shooting rats.

We found whiskey bottles hidden in both the basement and chicken coop. Once Tom and I took a swig and almost choked to death, then put a little water in the bottle. Tom said, "No wonder he's so mean all the time."

Anyway, Uncle Ned yelled right back at Gram. "These goddammed, snot nosed kids are up to something. Knocking goddammed pictures off the wall in the middle of the night."

"No need to curse. No need at all. Everyone, go back to bed," she yelled.

Uncle Ned took a step back and I could see his outline again. "I'll take care of you two in the morning," he said. I could tell he'd just been itching to hit us.

"Okay, Gram. Good night," I shouted, getting off the trunk and under the covers where it was a lot safer. I put the picture on the trunk.

"Snot nosed kids," he said as he left the room, slamming the door so hard it almost came off its hinges.

After he slammed the door to his own room and we felt safe again, Tom and I stuck our heads under the covers and started giggling. We couldn't help it. The danger had passed. We knew the mystery of the hole in the wall would probably never be solved. Gram wouldn't tell us. But she saved us again tonight, that's for sure.

"I can't wait till I get a little bigger," I said. I'm

gonna beat him up so bad ..."

"I'm gonna kill him someday," Tom said in a matter of fact way.

He wasn't whispering and we weren't giggling anymore.

I lay there awhile, thinking about things. Now just a sliver of moonlight was coming in, but it hit right on the picture on the trunk. Eerie looking. I was going to show it to Tom.

"Hey, Tom," I whispered. But it was too late. He was sleeping already.

From War To Peace

"When the war stopped, our lives went on pretty much the same. Uncle Ned was still acting crazy at times, Gram was still defending him, even as she made fun of him, and protecting us at the same time. We were still flushing the toilet with a hose, and Uncle Ned hadn't replaced the chain on the toilet upstairs or the rubber inner tube that took the place of a pipe elbow in the basement."

From War To Peace

All of us are walking history books, a mix of personal history that never makes the news interlaced with textbook history that becomes as much a part of us as our fingerprints.

For me, history was the start of the war and President Roosevelt's "Day of Infamy" speech; and the day Benny went into the Army; and the end of the war announcement which we heard from H.V. Kaltenborn, the radio newsman, our old nemesis who killed many a "Lone Ranger" episode.

The war meant meat rationing, but we had chickens, rabbits, and pigeons in the chicken coop, along with the rats. The rats got their share, but so did we. We had plenty of meat.

Sugar rationing didn't affect us, either, because Uncle Ned had been making sure we didn't eat too much sugar for as long as we could remember.

Tom and I didn't notice gasoline rationing much, either, because we walked to school and downtown, and sometimes walked about three miles over the boulevard, "The Skyline Drive" it was called, with our sled in the winter and our wagon in the summer to haul feed for the chickens and rabbits.

The war was awful from what we heard on the radio and saw in the newsreels, but it didn't change life for me and Tom that much. Our major worry was for Benny to get home okay.

Uncle Chuck, well, we hardly knew him before he went into the Army. We were reminded of him plenty of times with Gram always talking about Big Helen stealing the mail.

When the war stopped, our lives went on pretty much the same. Uncle Ned was still acting crazy at times, Gram was still defending him, even as she made fun of him, and protecting us at the same time. We were still flushing the toilet with a hose, and Uncle Ned hadn't replaced the chain on the toilet or the rubber inner tube that took the place of a pipe elbow in the basement.

Gram was still reciting her poems and sayings until we heard them all a thousand times, but every so often she'd pop a new one on us, like, "Cheer up, the worst is yet to come," which none of us ever figured out. We figured she made up that one when Uncle Chuck came home safe from the war and then stayed married to Big Helen.

For most people, life was returning to normal. For us, it just kept on the way it was except that Benny came home. That was a big deal for me and Tom, and it turned out to be an even bigger deal for Uncle Ned, but not the way he figured.

No one in our family was killed in the war. Benny made it home in the fall of 1945. Uncle Chuck, who was captured by the Germans in the Battle of the Bulge, also got home. Benny never talked about the war.

"Hey Benny," I'd say, "tell us what you did over there."

"Someday," he'd say.

"Did you ever meet General MacArthur?" I persisted.

"Yeah, once."

"Really? Wow! What did he say?"

"He said, 'Get out of my way.'"

And I knew Tom and I weren't going to hear any war stories, not then anyway.

Even though Benny never talked about the war, he did listen to our war stories about how Uncle Ned was always slapping us around. Then he made it a point to visit and ask Uncle Ned to come outside for a talk near the chicken coop.

Tom and I watched from the kitchen window. Benny had put on about 45 pounds in the Army, all muscle. Part of that muscle was now in Uncle Ned's face and it looked like Uncle Ned was saying, "Yeah, okay, okay," and anything he could to calm down our brother.

Benny came in and said, "I don't think he'll be

hitting you guys anymore." He went over and hugged Gram and told her everything was okay, then left because Marion, his childhood sweetheart and future wife, was waiting in the car.

So in the fall of 1945 we really didn't know our older brother much better than before he went to war, but we were as proud of him as if he'd defeated a Japanese battalion single-handed.

Uncle Ned came in later and went upstairs to his room and started showing himself home movies again. He still did crazy things like talking to the chickens, and he still got drunk all the time and kept doing that little sugar minuet to show us not to eat too much, but somewhere in the back of his head was our brother's warning and the red light that flashed in his head that day never turned off. We were safe.

"If a job is once begun ..."

"Oh, man, what had I gotten myself into? There must have been a hundred guys in the lobby. Some were skinny like me, shorter, taller, big husky guys, some looked like football players, and I didn't know any one except Bob Schumacher, who came up behind me and punched me real hard in the shoulder, like he was doing me a favor letting me know he was there."

"If a job is once begun ..."

I didn't read the paper much. I did like to read about the war, but when the war was over and Benny was home again, I didn't bother very often. One particular night, though, I did happen to read the paper — and I'm happy I did.

That night, Uncle Ned was being pleasant for a change. He even wore his new glass eye to supper. It made Tom and me sick when he would eat supper with just one eye.

I was feeling pretty good, so I picked up the newspaper after supper and started reading. I saw something in the paper that really got me excited: "Bob Gerber, Sports Columnist for the Duluth News Tribune will coach a Golden Gloves team. The last team from Duluth was active fighting opponents from the Iron Range and Twin Cities in 1940, but the sport was suspended during the war. Gerber, a former Golden Gloves fighter will hold tryouts tonight in the YMCA at the corner of Fourth Street and Mesabi Avenue. All weight divisions are open. The All City Tournament will be held at the Shrine Auditorium Feb. 16, 17 and 18. Everyone is welcome. Check at the YMCA desk tonight at 7:30 p.m."

Uncle Ned used to box, in ancient times, but I wasn't going to tell him I might want to try out. All he'd do is make fun of me and say I'd never make it because I was too much like Dad. So I waited till he went outside.

"Gram, listen."

I read the article to her.

"Think I could go?"

Gram didn't let us out after supper except to play football or baseball on Fifth Street or in the empty lot across the street. So she took a long time to answer.

"Go, but I want you home as soon as it's over. If you use this as an excuse to run around I'll put a stop to it just like that."

Gram tried to snap her fingers, but she couldn't make a sound. Her hands and wrists were all twisted from arthritis and her fingers just wouldn't snap. But I got the point.

"I promise I'll be home as soon as it's over."

Gram paused, then said, "Go. If you're gonna be a fighter, be a good one."

"Can I go?" Tom asked, knowing what the answer would be.

"No, you're too young. It's time for you to go to bed anyway. Now, get up there."

"Aw, Grammmmmmm!" Tom said in a whine only he could get away with. Being the youngest, he was Gram's pet.

After a hug from Gram, he got one more shot at me. "You lucky creep," he said. Then he punched me in the arm and sulked up the stairs to our room, bouncing against the walls with every step.

Gram turned to me and said, "Once you start, keep at it." And then after a pause, "If a job is once begun, never leave it till it's done." Two of her sayings in one breath.

"Yeah, I know Gram." I started to leave, but turned and said, "I won't quit."

"I know you won't" she said, pulling my head down to her face so she could give me a kiss. I couldn't tell if she believed me or not, but I was going to make it — just to show Uncle Ned, if nothing else. Maybe I could shut him up about my dad running away.

I yelled, "See ya later" to Gram and ran down Ninth Avenue West, the steep hill bordering the front of our house.

The street lights were on, although it was not really dark yet, even the one on the corner that got shot out or broken from rocks so many times. That was the one that cast flickering mountain ash leaf shadows across our bedroom walls and helped us sleep on summer nights when we figured there was still so much playing time left. It was the light Gram called her "street corner moon," and it threw those same shadows through the screened-in porch where Gram sat singing to herself quietly, not knowing we could hear her sometimes when we were falling asleep. I hoped the street light would still be in one piece by the time I get home because it was going to be dark by then.

Ninth Avenue was good for roadwork. I could run it twice a night back and forth to the YMCA and four times a day for school because I went home for lunch. I was going to get into such good shape no one was ever going to beat me just by tiring me out.

I hadn't even gotten to the "Y" yet, and there I was talking about never getting beat. Maybe I wouldn't even make the team. Maybe I would get beat up so bad in the gym I would never want to get into the ring in the first place. Lots of guys never make it to the ring.

I had never been inside the YMCA. It was a big place that looked like a jail. I got to the big double doors and pulled hard to get one open. "If I have to work this hard to get the door open, how am I ever gonna be a fighter?" I asked myself.

Oh, man, what had I gotten myself into? There must have been a hundred guys in the lobby. Some were skinny like me, shorter, taller, big husky guys, some looked like football players, and I didn't know any one except Bob Schumacher, who came up behind me and punched me real hard in the shoulder, like he was doing me a favor letting me know he was there.

He was the kid who had failed in school about a hundred times and was at least three years older than the rest of us, but still in the eighth grade. Not too stupid, but I wasn't going to tell him how stupid I thought he was until I got in better shape because he was always the toughest kid in the room. Of course, who wouldn't be if they were three years older than all the other guys?

So, of all the people who showed up, he had to be one of them. He was the one I was in training for, so he showed up and punched me on the arm as though he was glad to see me. He just knew for sure there was one guy here he could beat up on ... so far. I had to add the "so far" because what was the sense of learning boxing if you couldn't get good enough to beat up someone who has been beating up on you all the time?

Like Uncle Ned. Someday, after I had a lot of fights and put on some weight, he was going to get it. "Bam," right on the jaw someday. He would never expect it because he had been punching us around and getting away with it for so long — until Benny warned him about it just a couple months earlier. First I had to learn some things about boxing.

But now it looked as though I would have to be sparring Bob Schumacher because we weighed about the same. "Hey, how you doing?" I said after he punched me on the arm like I'm his best friend, one he can beat up whenever he wants to. You wouldn't punch someone that hard when you first saw him unless you knew you could beat him up.

"Pretty good," he said. "What're you doing here?" He asked the question in a way that made it sound like a big surprise that I should be there. He forgot I was always the second toughest kid in the room, which should mean something.

"I'm gonna learn to box," I said.

"Huh!" he says, as if the idea sounded ridiculous.

"Well, I'm gonna do it," I said, trying to convince Schumacher and myself at the same time.

"Hey, shut up," he said, "Looks like the guy wants to say something."

The guy he was talking about wasn't very big or tough looking, and he was not that much older than some of the guys in the lobby, but he was telling us to head downstairs to the gym after we signed some papers. I had already signed, so I started downstairs with Schumacher and a lot of the other guys .

The stairs were pretty dark and a couple of us tripped on the way down.

"You'd think they'd turn the lights on, wouldn't you?" I said to Schumacher, just to have something to say as we walked.

"Lights are for sissys," he said. Just his way of keeping one up on me, I figured.

I decided I would always pretend his face was on the punching bag. And some day I would get him. That would be the end of this smart guy, Schumacher.

We separated as we entered the training room. It had a big vault door that slid open and let us into a huge room with a ring at the far end and a couple of heavy bags and small punching bags already up, jump ropes hanging from hooks on the wall, adhesive tape rolls and boxing gloves all over the place. There were no chairs, though, so everyone was standing around when the guy started talking again.

"My name's Gerber. Bob Gerber. Me and my friend, Bob Burke, are going to be your trainers. Both of us fought Golden Gloves and AAU. I don't know how many of you will stick it out, but only eight of you will make the team. Bob and me will see to it that the best ones make it. It'll be a tough schedule and you need to stick to the training program we set up. Got it?" he asked.

And there were a lot of "Yeah, yeah" answers and hands going up, as though they were all going to be the final eight. I put one arm up, the arm Schumacher hit, but I didn't say, "Yeah, yeah" because I was not so sure I was in the right place.

Gerber was no bigger than Father Logan. Father is our principal at school and one of the toughest priests anywhere, next to Monsignor Lynch. Father Logan can shut up Schumacher in a second, and all the football players, too. I got the feeling Gerber was just like Father Logan. Just something about the way he talked — like someone who knows what he's talking about.

And Burke, man, he was like Gerber's bodyguard.

Big and really tough looking, with a face that must have been run over by a truck. He looked like he could chew up Father Logan and Gerber at the same time.

Gerber told us to get into our tennies and sweat suits, if we brought them along. "And if you didn't bring your tennis shoes along, take off your shoes and socks and work out in your bare feet," Burke said. Burke didn't bother explaining we had to do that so we wouldn't mark up the gym floor. It was clear he didn't think he had to explain anything. He expected us to just do what he said.

I got into my tennies and noticed Schumacher didn't bring his, so he was in his bare feet. We started some stretching exercises, and both Burke and Gerber did them with us. Gerber looked to be in good shape. Burke had so many muscles that he could barely stretch, but who was going to say anything?

"Let's do some push ups," Burke said. "I don't want any excuses." If your feet slip, dig your toenails in the floor." It's a hardwood floor, so I laughed about it along with a lot of other guys who knew Burke was joking, but not Schumacher. That was another thing about him. You couldn't joke with Schumacher because he never got the point.

Now Gerber took over again. "Get some space between you and the next guy" he said. "I'm going to show you some basics about boxing. How to stand so you don't trip over yourself, how to throw a left jab, the most important punch in boxing, and how to throw a straight right hand. Nothing else tonight, just those three things. Okay, here's how you stand."

The rest of the night he showed us those three things, and Burke was going around the room helping out. At the end of the workout, Gerber said, "Tomorrow we'll have more of this and, later in the week, I'll show you how to hit the heavy bag. It won't be long before you'll know a lot more than the average guy on the street. But I want you to remember something. Never use anything I teach you here except in the boxing ring. We don't want any bullies pushing people around on the street or in the school yard." And then he told us to show up tomorrow night at the same time.

It was too late for him to mention the "bullies" thing to Schumacher. He had been a bully since the fourth grade, when he started failing. He had left already, so I headed out the vault door towards Ninth Avenue and ran home. I couldn't wait to tell Gram and Tom. I thought I was going to like it. Hitting that heavy bag was going to be the fun part, especially when I thought of Schumacher's face on it.

Coming Home

I ran home from that first night of boxing, racing up Ninth Avenue to the wooden sidewalk leading to our house, up the three wooden steps, and into the screened-in porch.

Our mailmen walked that same route, onto the wooden sidewalk, up those wooden steps, never knowing if their approach to the locked mailbox on the porch would be met by a ferocious lunge from Mickey. Mickey terrified everyone who approached — meter readers, scissors sharpeners, even kids who were our friends.

Gram, for the first time, took the pose that would welcome me home from all my fights ... the fighter's pose, fists doubled as best she could with her arthritis, hands up, stance extended, looking like she could have handled half the guys who showed up that night.

"How'd you do?" she asked.

"It's too early to tell, Gram. Lots of guys, and we just went through some of the basic moves."

Her fighter's stance turned into a hug. Then she

said, "If you're gonna fight at all, fight like Mickey."

"What do you mean, 'If I fight at all?'" I asked.

"If you're gonna stick it out," she said.

It sounded like she was harping on me about my Dad again.

"There must'a been a hundred guys there, Gram," I said.

"Once they start hitting each other, count 'em again," she said.

"What do you mean?"

"Many of 'em won't be back once they see what it's really like."

"Gram, you don't know anything about boxing."

"All four of my boys boxed when they were young, and they all told the same story. Lots of 'em showed up at first until the hitting started, then they dropped out, one by one."

"Well, Gerber said only eight of us would make the team," I said.

"Who's Gerber?"

"He's one of the coaches."

"So?"

"Anyway, he said only eight of us would make the team, one guy in each weight division."

"Does that mean Gerber will only let eight of you in the gym once the team is chosen?"

"No, Gram, I'm sure he wants sparring partners and all that."

"So you're gonna be one of those who stick it out, even if you don't make the team?"

"Yeah, yeah. I wanna make the team, but, if I don't, I'll still stick around and be a sparring partner." I knew I was digging a deep hole for myself, but Gram kept leading me on.

"And you're gonna fight like Mickey?" she asked.

"Yeah, Gram, just like Mickey." Mickey was ferocious, I didn't think I was ferocious, but she got me saying it.

"I'm gonna go to bed," I said.

"Tommy's up there and he's probably still awake, wantin' to know what happened."

"Yeah."

"Don't talk too long. You gotta get up bright and early tomorrow."

I headed for the kitchen ready to go upstairs, but stopped when Gram said, "Big Helen stole the mail again today."

"You're kidding. She'd never get past Mickey."

"She's got a key to the mailbox, I just know it."

"Gram, in the first place, where would she have gotten a key? And how could she come on the porch without Mickey biting her? And you were home all day, so you'd have heard her anyway."

"She's a devil, Bobby, that's the only way I can explain it."

"What? Mickey would take her leg off."

"She's a devil, I tell you. Now go to bed."

"Gram, you get me started with talk about Big Helen stealing the mail, then you tell me to go to bed, like nothing happened."

"All I know is she was here today," she said. "Are you keeping your bedroom clean?" she asked as an afterthought.

"Yeah, Gram," I said.

Arthritis kept Gram from climbing the stairs to our bedroom, so she didn't know the plaster wall on Tom's side of the bed crumbled last summer, leaving the exposed lath. It was okay in the summer, but in the winter it was like having a window open.

It was our fault because we'd shoot our BB guns at clay soldiers set up on the bed and, when we missed, the BB would make a pock mark on the wall. One day a single BB hit the wall, "the last straw," as Gram would say, and caused an entire section of plaster to fall.

Gram also didn't know that layers of magazines littered the floor.

The wall at the far end of our room was stacked to the ceiling with boxes of Good Housekeeping and Ring magazines. It was fun to read stories of the old time fighters like Fritzie Zivic, the dirtiest fighter of all time, who was a master at spinning his opponent so the referee couldn't see him, then thumbing the poor guy in the eyes or heeling him in the face with the laces of his gloves. I wasn't going to fight like Fritzie Zivic, but he was Tom's and my secret hero for some reason we couldn't understand and didn't try to explain to Gram. We knew she'd have a poem about it.

We could never figure out who read Good Housekeeping, but we loved to read old Ring magazines. Our fumbling for old issues weakened the boxes. Slowly and silently magazines flowed across the floor until the door barely opened wide enough for us to get in and out.

Gram almost made it upstairs one dark winter morning when we were ignoring her repeated calls to get up for school. I happened to look in the direction of the grain barrel on the landing and saw a ghostly face with long gray hair floating there in the half-light, seemingly unattached to a body. It was Gram, making a supreme effort to get upstairs. But it was as far as she ever got, and she never saw the mess.

Gram kept her long hair in a bun during the day, but at night she'd let it fall loose. She had just done that after her comment about Big Helen and was trying to brush her hair, but each time she raised her arm she made a face that showed the pain she felt from her arthritis.

"Here, let me help," I said. We both moved to the screened-in porch and Gram sat in the rocking chair opposite the mailbox . She handed me the brush and I started brushing her hair.

It was turning into a good night. I never expected Gram's welcome, and felt good about it. Besides, I thought I'd like boxing. I knew I'd have to stick it out because of hearing about my dad all the time, so I was glad I liked it.

We didn't talk at first and Gram started humming "Rock of Ages." To top it off, Mickey was sitting there getting petted by Gram, like a normal dog — a dog that never got hit twice and hurt bad chasing cars, or that didn't almost hang himself by his own chain when he fell through the second story steps of Rigstad's corner grocery and was standing there on his back legs trying to breath when we found him, or that didn't love to bite people and fight other dogs regardless of their size.

Gram must have forgotten about Big Helen stealing the mail, and the rats in the chicken coop killing the pigeons and rabbits, and whether it was finally going to rain so the garden wouldn't shrivel up, and even about me going to bed so I could get up in the morning.

So there I was, brushing Gram's hair, feeling good, not knowing why, at least not so as I could explain it to anyone. And Gram just sitting there, humming and singing with her "street corner moon" flickering light and leaf shadows all over the place.

Have You Ever Boxed Before?

"I could barely stand up by the time the bell rang. The referee separated us and helped me back to my corner. Referees usually don't do that."

Have You Ever Boxed Before?

Explaining to someone who has never fought in the ring how it feels to fight in the ring is difficult, but I will try.

Did you ever have a dream that someone was trying to kill you and you yelled to all the people standing near you, but no one heard or tried to help? In one of my fights, that's what it was like.

I won my first fight and even remember my opponent's name after all this time — Dan Raymond, a skinny kid like me, weighing 112 pounds. We were called "flyweights," the smallest weight class in boxing.

In that first fight, I was exhausted after three rounds and so was poor Dan. I knocked him down once, and maybe that's why I won. But I was all flailing arms. I had no real boxing skills, but I must have landed more punches than Dan, and I didn't get knocked down.

My fourth fight was the one like the bad dream of someone trying to kill you and all the people standing around. Naturally, the guy who was trying to kill me was

Bob Schumaker.

After winning that first fight I lost the next two, so now I had a lousy record of one win and two losses. And then I had to fight Schumaker. The Duluth paper ran my picture posing in my gloves and trunks and made the mistake of putting Bob Schumaker's name under it. He was really mad about that, although I had nothing to do with it. He told me he was going to kill me for that alone. I wasn't too thrilled about the picture mistake either because he was homely on top of being stupid, but I didn't want to kill him or anyone else because of it. Right before the fight he also told me he didn't like me all those years when he was toughest kid in the room and I was second toughest. So it was pretty much of a grudge match, at least from his side.

I had my own cheering section with Benny, Tom, and my sister Al, and they had ringside seats. Benny paid for all the seats. He didn't really know anything about Schumaker. He just figured that, after losing two fights, I could use some cheering from the ringside seats. And he was right.

Al brought a rosary along and showed it to me before the fight, as if that was going to help. The only other time I saw a rosary at an event was at a funeral when I was an altar boy, so it didn't exactly cheer me up.

In my first three fights, I hadn't been knocked down. In fact I hadn't been hurt at all, just exhausted. I was still a tangle of arms and legs and hadn't shown much boxing skill, though Gerber assured me I was getting better. Both the fights I lost were close, and Gerber told me they could have gone either way.

I felt good about the Schumaker fight. I had been punching the big bag pretty well and I was hitting it right in the spot where I had put Schumaker's face.

The bell rang for the first round, and I did okay. I was fresh and held my own. Every time I landed a punch I could hear Benny yelling, "Kill him, Bobby, kill him." Well, I knew he didn't really mean I should "kill him," but hearing Benny yell anything cheered me up.

The Shrine Auditorium held 1,500 people and it was packed, yet I could hear Benny over all the crowd. And he didn't just yell, he'd get up and wave his arms so the people behind him probably had trouble seeing, but that didn't bother Benny when he got excited.

I started tiring in the second round and Schumaker landed a good one that knocked me down before the bell rang. I went down near my corner, so I didn't have far to go to reach the stool and get some water and instructions. Gerber passed smelling salts under my nose to perk me up, and it worked.

Except for the knockdown, I thought I might be winning. Benny was yelling, "Get 'em Bobby, get 'em." Of course, we both were named Bobby, but I'm sure Schumaker heard it and knew what my brother meant. He wasn't that stupid.

He came roaring at me when the bell rang for the

third round. But I was ready for that goon and tore out of my corner at him. The smelling salts helped, and hearing Benny yelling all through the minutes rest helped, too. We almost collided in the middle of the ring.

I was doing okay at first, but he caught me a good one that staggered me. I got a numb feeling in my brain, like when someone wakes you from a deep sleep and you don't know where you are right away. I moved back, hoping to get away from him for a few seconds until I could think straight again. But he was on me before I knew it and I was on the floor again.

I managed to get up, but the referee could see I wasn't in great shape, so he counted to eight before he let me fight again. Schumaker couldn't wait to get at me again. Talk about a "killer instinct," he had it.

Benny was yelling, "Get him, Bobby, get him." He wasn't using the word "kill" any more because he probably figured that, if someone were going to be killed, it might be me. But that didn't stop Benny from yelling like mad.

Schumaker was throwing haymakers now, hoping to knock me out, but most of them were missing. The trouble was one landed and I went down. I didn't even feel the punch. That's what happens when you get hit on the tip of the chin. By the time the referee counted "three," I knew I was on the floor. And I was lying right in front of my cheering section.

All three of them were out of their seats yelling. I

couldn't tell at first what they were saying, but I knew it must be about getting up. While they were jumping up and down, I felt like I could just lie there and go to sleep for a couple hours.

The biggest thing that helped me get up was my Sister Al. She was crying and waving what was left of her rosary in my face. I found out later she had torn it into about five pieces during the fight. Lying on the floor, I couldn't even tell it was a rosary until I saw the cross dangling from her clenched fist.

I got up and Schumaker was all over me. I was trying to punch back, but not doing a good job of it. My arms didn't seem like they were connected to my shoulders anymore. Schumaker was landing some good ones, Benny was yelling, but, as in the dream I mentioned, he had to stay where he was.

I could barely stand up by the time the bell rang. The referee separated us and helped me back to my corner. Referees usually don't do that. I lost the fight. Going down three times didn't help, even though I was doing okay until that first knockdown.

Still I felt pretty good when Benny bought us ice cream cones later. Al said, "Have you ever thought about taking up some other sport, Bobby? I don't have any rosaries left." It was Al's idea of a joke and would have been funnier if I hadn't already thought about it. But, if I quit, Benny would never talk to me again.

And Uncle Ned and Gram, well, I'd never hear the

end of it. It would prove to Uncle Ned I was just like my dad. So I didn't give it much thought and just finished my ice cream cone and walked home with Tom.

Gram was waiting in her fighter's stance. And she asked the same question she always asked, "Did you knock him out?"

I got a big hug from Gram when she heard the story of the fight. She even hugged Tom, and all he did was cheer. Hugs were scarce at Gram's house, but they always felt good. And this one really felt good.

Dad Comes Home

"Tom and I both knew Dad had been in town for a couple of weeks, staying at Benny's house. Gram knew it, too, and dreaded seeing or talking to him. He hadn't called until today. It didn't seem strange to us that Dad tacked on two more weeks to the thirteen years he had already been gone. Or that neither of us were eager to meet him."

Dad Comes Home

Gram answered the phone in an angry voice and said, "Come if you must," then slammed the receiver down so hard it must have rattled both ear drums of the person at the other end.

The receiver on those phones worked so a person could either slip it back on the hook and depress it gently or really slam it down so the other person knew how you felt — BANG! "Take that!"

I was pretty sure I knew who was on the other end even before Gram said, "That dirty Irish rotter is coming to see the boys," but I asked her anyway.

"Was that my dad?"

"Want me to stop him, Ma?" It was Uncle Ned.

"No, he has a right to see 'em, I know that," Gram said. Then she quickly added, "But he's not gonna stick one 'dirty Irish rotter foot in this house," as if "Irish rotter" was not only part of his name, but covered all his body parts too.

Tom and I both knew Dad had been in town for a

couple of weeks, staying at Benny's house. Gram knew it, too, and dreaded seeing or talking to him. He hadn't called until today. It didn't seem strange to us that Dad tacked on two more weeks to the thirteen years he had already been gone. Or that neither of us were eager to meet him. Dad wouldn't be able to see Tom today because Uncle Hank had taken him to the Duluth Dukes baseball game.

"If it's upsetting you so much, just let me stop him." It was Uncle Ned again.

"No, no. I told you he has a right. I don't want any more foolishness and fighting. We've had enough of that already."

Uncle Ned went upstairs to his bedroom. But his second offer to "stop our dad from coming" seemed to calm Gram and she said, "I'll let him come in, Bobby, but take him outside and do your talking."

"Okay," I said, wondering what we were going to be talking about anyway. Gram started a pot of coffee on the kitchen stove. I started shadow boxing to get rid of the nervous energy that was building up. The coffee was barely finished when we heard the knock on the door.

Gram answered and without a "hello," said, "Harry, this is Bobby."

He was bigger than I was and still wiry, the way he looked in all the old pictures, and his hair was still black. He didn't seem insulted by Grams' introduction.

I said, "Hi," as if it didn't matter.

His handshake was strong. He smiled and said, "Hello, Son," in a warm voice and my knees almost buckled. He called me "Son." I don't know why, but I didn't expect that. Gram went to her bedroom. I said, "Maybe we can go outside and talk." Dad agreed and we moved through the screened-in porch, past Gram's rocking chair and the locked mailbox, to the front steps where we both sat down. He was graceful in his movements, and I figured he was probably a pretty good fighter, as everyone said. I was nervous and stumbled over Gram's rocker, but he pretended not to notice.

"Well, Bobby, it's good to see you again." he said.

"Yeah," I answered nervously.

"How's school going," he asked.

"Okay," I said.

What grade you in?

"Eleventh." There was a pause and I added, "I've been boxing for a couple of years."

"Terrific! Yeah, I know. Benny told me about it. What weight?"

"Lightweight," I answered.

I tried hard to feel something — anger, happiness, excitement — but I couldn't. We talked of ordinary things, even the weather. Yet there were so many things I could have said and so many questions I could have asked, but didn't. I could have asked him, "Why did you leave?" and "Did you ever think about us and wonder how we were doing?" But I didn't.

I should have been angry for all the telegrams that read, "Will send money soon. Regards, Harry." because Gram said the money never came. I should have at least asked him about that, for Gram's sake. Gram had lots of those telegrams and showed them to us once in a while to remind us "what a dirty Irish rotter" he was, in case we had forgotten.

It was impossible to argue with Gram. What could we say? Deep down, we always thought to ourselves, "He can't be that bad." Now, meeting him, I was thinking, "He ain't that bad."

Maybe he wouldn't have left after only an hour, but Gram came out and said, "Bobby has chores to do, Harry. You'd better go now." She said it gently, but with a restrained fury, as if she had a wet dishrag in both hands just ready to let loose.

So this man who used to go into a bar and announce, "I'll fight any Swede in the place" and was so wiry he could run up the wall of his favorite tavern and almost reach the ceiling before he came down again, left quietly. "Yeah, maybe it's time to go." he said. He didn't shake hands this time. He gave me a gentle punch on the shoulder, said, "I'll see you again, Son," and left. My mom called me "Son" in that long ago dream, but never again until that day had I heard that word. And then I heard it twice in an hour.

So I helped Gram feed the rabbits and chickens, and neither of us said anything about his visit that day or at any time after that, as though it never happened.

Go If You Must

"But her favorite daughter had just been buried, and she blamed him then, and blamed him the rest of her life. So, maybe the scene wasn't that peaceful, and maybe it didn't happen that way at all."

Go If You Must

I have only one other memory of my dad, and it's like a slow motion scene in an old home movie, full of haze and doubt.

My mother's funeral was over. I was three years old. My older sisters told me years later that I didn't know my father as well as I knew my mother. From what they told me, I had been my mother's constant companion, and that had left an imprint, a presence felt, more than a memory of specific times. I saw my father far less, because he worked long hours and often stayed out drinking after work.

But I have one memory. I was in the bedroom that eventually became Tom's and mine, and my shoulders were pressed against the mattress while my dad was talking. He wore an overcoat that made him look even bigger than he was, and he hunched down to be closer and held out his arms for me to come to him. Instead, I turned to Gram and hugged her leg. She reached down and picked me up and I hugged her around her neck with my back to my father.

I don't remember crying or talking or Gram saying anything, yet there must have been words. My dad
must have said, "Come with me, Bobby, come along,
Son." And Gram may have softened my rejection by
saying, "Let him stay with his brothers and sisters. He's
frightened now. Go if you must. Maybe it'll be different
when you come back."

But her favorite daughter had just been buried,
and she blamed him then, and blamed him the rest of her
life. So, maybe the scene wasn't that peaceful, and
maybe it didn't happen that way at all. I was only three,
so I can't be sure what happened. I never asked Gram if
it happened that way, or if it happened at all. It's a foggy
scene recalled imperfectly from a distance of decades,
explored now through layers of time and experience
with powers of reason and logic and written words as
tools to sort and untangle vague memories.

But I know this much. When Dad visited 13 years
later, Mickey didn't growl, threaten, snarl, or bite him.

Later Tom and I talked about it and couldn't figure
it out. Over the years, Mickey had pretty much bitten or
nipped all the family members once or twice and had torn
the pants and opened wounds on more than one mailman
or delivery man. But for some reason he was unusually
friendly to Dad.

So, if Mickey, the toughest dog in Duluth sensed
something about my dad and gave him a pass, maybe I

can, too. Maybe I can remember him not from the empty telegrams and the endless bad stories from Gram, but with the gentle punch on my shoulder and those last words, "See you again, Son."

Saved By Uncle Ned

I couldn't believe it. Gram actually broke down and let me go to a party, knowing it wouldn't get over until midnight. Of course, I was 16 now and had been traveling to places like Fargo and St. Cloud and staying overnight for boxing matches with the Duluth team. So she was getting used to me being on my own once in a while. The other reason was the party was only a few houses down the street.

It was at the home of Fred and Betty Johnson, nice people Gram liked. They weren't going to be home, but she didn't know that, and I wasn't going to tell her.

Ron Johnson was throwing the party. He made a good impression on grownups, but us guys in the neighborhood knew better. Ron was the first guy to smoke, the first one to go out on a date with a girl, and the first one to sleep with a girl — which he told us about in great detail. He was also the best football and baseball player among us. And he could tell lies and get away with it. Ron was our hero.

So when he told us he was going to have a party Friday night and only invited six of us, we knew it was really going to be something. "Don't worry about the girls," he said. "I'll supply 'em." He acted as if he had a whole warehouse full of girls, so we didn't worry. "I've got plenty of good stuff to drink, so don't worry about that either" he said. "Just get your ass over here by eight o'clock sharp."

I felt good that he included me. Gram was always strict about us going out at night, so the guys almost stopped inviting us for anything. I tried not to show my excitement about it or Gram would get suspicious. I'd never been on a date. Geraldine was finally talking to me again, but that's all it was, talk. Gram warned me a couple of times, "Now if there's any drinking going on, you come right home." I figured Ron wasn't going to have us drink lemonade with a house full of girls and his parents gone, but I just said, "Okay Gram." As I reached the outer screen door, she got in one more warning, "Lips that touch liquor shall never touch mine." I jumped down all four steps.

I walked into Ron's house and there were open liquor bottles all over the place. And girls — they were all over the place, too. Ron poured me a glass with some whiskey and lots of ice. His girlfriend was a real cute blond, the cutest one at the party, natch! He offered me the drink in front of her, so I figured I'd show off a little. "More whiskey, less ice," I said, braver now because his girl was sort of smiling at me as though she wanted Ron to introduce us. Ron gave me the glass and said, "Take it nice and slow," as if I needed him to be my counselor.

"Come here." He motioned to a girl standing by the sink. I was hoping this wasn't my girl because she had stringy hair, thick glasses, and was skinny. "Bobby, meet Gladys," he said. She came over and seemed nice enough, but I kept thinking, "I should have known. Ron gets the best looking one and I get stuck with the ugliest girl in the room, probably in the whole city. That's why he invited me. All the other guys know about her from other parties. She's friendly with Ron's' girl and I figured they're best friends, and where Ron's girl goes, Gladys goes. I hadn't even heard Ron's girlfriend's name yet.

We said, "Hi" and I immediately took a big gulp of my drink and started choking. Everyone started laughing, even Gladys, and I noticed she wasn't so homely when she smiled. Ron poured some more whiskey into my glass and tried to make me feel better by saying, "Hey you two, join me and Penny over here." He put his arm on my shoulder like I was his great old buddy, but he hadn't even introduced me to Penny. He didn't have to invite me twice, and I made sure I sat opposite Penny.

I finished off the drink even before I sat down and said in a pretty loud voice to make up for the choking, "Hey this stuff's like lemonade." Since I was sitting on the inside of the kitchen booth, Ron got me another drink, but had the same warning, "Nice and slow ...." He was starting to sound like Gram.

Just then I felt something on my ankle. I was about to look under the table when I caught the look on Penny's face and could tell it was her bare foot. I'd have looked pretty stupid looking under the table. That had never happened to me before and it felt terrific. I couldn't even describe it. Ron was pouring me another drink, so I slipped off my shoes and put my feet around hers. Wow!

Ron brought the drink back — no cubes this time. And he wasn't stupid, I think he was figuring out something was going on. He pulled Penny by the hand and started dancing even as they left the booth. He was really smooth with women. I was left with Gladys, so I took a big gulp and asked her if she wanted to dance. I didn't know how to dance and wasn't sure what I was going to do out there. But she was pretty good about it and took the lead and I don't think anyone noticed.

I can't remember much else until I woke up having to throw up. I was sitting on the couch, all the lights were out, and Gladys had her head on my lap. I got up so fast she went flying on the floor. I hadn't even used the bathroom, so I didn't know where it was. So I ran from room to room, flipping on light switches and making myself real popular. I never did find the bathroom, but found the door outside — where I threw up,

real loud. Boy, what a mess. And who comes out, but
Ron. He says, "Hey, sober up," and starts slapping me
in the face. I was always proud that I could take a good
punch when I was boxing, but here I was on the ground
from a slap. I couldn't believe it. A slap and I'm down.
I got up and threw up again and said, "Yeah, I think I'd
better go home."

"Yeah, I think so." And he slapped me one more
time. This time I didn't go down and yelled at him..
"Hey, watch it."

"Look, you dumb ass, you're drunk and your
Gram is going to kill you and then she'll tell my mom and
dad and then what?" This was the first party he had ever
asked me to and now he's saying, "And then what?" As
if it would all be my fault. "Hey, I'm sorry." I said.
"Come back in. I'll put on some coffee." After about
five cups of coffee, I was still sick, but I figured I'd better
get home.

I left and started walking fifth street to Gram's
house. I was going to cut through the field by the flower
garden and sneak in the back door, but when I got close,
I could hear Gram yelling at someone. I was too far away
so I knew she wasn't yelling at me. And then I saw it.
Uncle Ned was hanging on the hood of his Diamond T
truck, drunk as anything, throwing up all over Gram's
flower garden, and Gram was hitting him with a towel
and yelling like crazy.

I went around the alley and came in the front door

and went right upstairs. Gram never said a word to me. Never smelled my breath. Here I was saved by Uncle Ned, and he never knew it.

College? What Is It?

"My scholastic record was terrible. I had taken every shop course possible: woodworking, printing, even cooking, where I made a baking powder biscuit that broke a window at school. I was poorly prepared for college and was to graduate sixty-third out of 96 students. Education wasn't highly regarded in our family, except by Gram, who had only gone to the eighth grade, and Aunt May, who almost became a nun. Tom and I always thought of school as a way to get into a few fights, and get out of the house."

College? What Is It?

One Saturday after a boxing workout, Gerber asked me to stick around. He took me to the YMCA lounge upstairs and didn't say anything at first, so I asked him, "Is anything wrong?" He said, "No, but I want to talk to you about something." I figured it had something to do with boxing.

"I've known you a couple of years now," he said. "You're coming along great in boxing, but I happen to know you're not doing that great in school." He had never mentioned my schoolwork before and I figured it wasn't something he'd be interested in. He didn't give me a chance to say anything before he went on. "Burke and I've been talking, and we both think you'd have a great chance to get a boxing scholarship to college."

I had fought two seasons on the Duluth Golden Gloves team, winning 19 and losing 5. I wasn't exactly Olympic material, but Gerber and Burke thought I was good enough to get a scholarship.

I was always courteous with Gerber. I liked him

as a coach and as a terrific person, but I blurted out, "Why would I ever want to go to college? I hate going to high school."

"I know that," he said. "That's why I wanted to talk to you about it first." He spent the next forty minutes telling me what college was and what it would do for me. "This could be one of the most important decisions of your life," was the way he put it, and he looked very serious. That got my attention.

He told me how he and Burke had both gone to college, how much fun it was, how they had met their wives in college, how the studying wasn't that bad. He made it sound like it wasn't a four year sentence to the penitentiary, which was the way I had always pictured it.

I was starting to get interested. "You'll meet girls, different from the ones in high school," he assured me, "and you'll have a chance to box all over the country. A lot of good things about it, Bobby, and it will prepare you for a much better life than the one you're heading into." I had been working part time at St. Germain's, a paint and wallpaper store in Duluth, and was hoping to become a floor clerk, or maybe work in their warehouse. I was intrigued and asked Gerber, "What should I do?"

"I've had some long conversations with Fr. Logan," he said, "and he thinks you still have time to improve your grades enough to get into a college on some sort of probationary deal. And he told me he'd write a letter to help. Then it would be up to you." I didn't even think Father Logan knew me. As principal, he had to be tough to keep everyone in line, so I stayed out of his way.

My scholastic record was terrible. I had taken every shop course possible: woodworking, printing, even cooking, where I made a baking powder biscuit that broke a window at school. I was poorly prepared for college and was to graduate sixty-third out of 96 students. Education wasn't highly regarded in our family, except by Gram, who had only gone to the eighth grade, and Aunt May, who almost became a nun. Tom and I always thought of school as a way to get into a few fights, and get out of the house.

"Bobby, you may not know it, but at some colleges, boxing is a major sport," Gerber said. The University of Wisconsin, for example, gets anywhere from 8,000 to 10,000 people at intercollegiate fights and up to 13,000 when the NCAA Championships are held in Madison."

"Wow!" I said. The Shrine Auditorium in Duluth only held 1,200 people.

Gerber was not only my coach, I trusted him. When I listened to him tell me what to do when he was in my corner, I usually won the fight. Maybe he knew what he was talking about on this college thing.

I didn't know it, but Gerber had also met with Sister Rose Marie, the toughest teacher in school. She taught English, my only favorite subject besides shop. I

liked her and found myself doing homework and volun-
teering answers in class, something I didn't do in any
other class. And she said to me one day, "You have the
ability to get through college. Don't pass up this chance."

Gram was letting me stay up later at night to do
homework.

There was an energy building, and it all pointed to
a scholarship.

I thought about it. College had girls. It was
somewhere else. It was beginning to sound like it could
be fun. I didn't like the thought of leaving Tom behind,
but even he was for it. Although Tom was three years
younger he was a better street fighter than I was, even
with his crippled left arm. He could throw a terrific left
hook, but couldn't jab at all. In the ring, that would make
him a one-armed fighter, a handicap no one could
overcome, so I knew he'd never get a college boxing
scholarship.

Gerber finally did it. After writing dozens of
letters, he arranged a boxing scholarship to The University of Wisconsin in Madison. Father Logan wrote the
letter that allowed me to get into the University, "On
Condition," as they called it, which meant I'd have to do
well in my grades right away, or I'd be out of school with
no second chance.

When I left for the University in the fall of 1950,
Gram was having to use a wheel chair because she had
broken her hip and it wasn't healing as it should. But she

still kept the chickens and rabbits and planned on keeping the garden. Tom would help, I knew that. But Uncle Ned was drinking heavier now and wasn't going to be much help.

I'd be 18 that December. Tom was 15. Gram was 78. Tom and I didn't know how old Uncle Ned was and didn't care. When we were growing up, we always thought he was about 50, but he looked older now and we both thought he was shrinking. He was still moody, still pouty, still threatening suicide once in a while.

Uncle Ned wished me luck and we shook hands. I had never shaken hands with him before. He was drinking and mellow now, but I knew his moods changed so fast it might not last through the handshake. He seemed happy for me.

Before leaving I got lots of advice.

"Go to Church," Gram said.

"Watch out for the communists on campus," Sister Rose Marie said.

"I don't want to see you back here working at St. Germain's," Father Logan said.

"I'm a phone call away," Gerber said.

"I'll be coming down there in a couple years," Tom said.

Gerber drove me to the station and Tom came along. We had time to sit around and talk before the bus loaded. As we talked, the foghorns were blasting away at each other, adding to the scared feeling I already had.

Tom and Gerber waved goodbye as the bus pulled out and there I was, waving back, with a scholarship waiting for me, a chance to fight in front of big crowds, an opportunity of a lifetime, and there was only one goofy thought going through my head: "I'm sure glad Madison doesn't have foghorns."

Madison

"My first year was a proving time, for grades and for boxing. And as far as girls, Gerber was right. They were a lot different than the ones in high school who wouldn't even talk to me."

Madison

I arrived in Madison about 8:00 p.m. and was met at the bus station by Warren Jollymore. "Jolly," as he was known by his friends, was a friend of Bob Gerber, from Proctor, a small town outside of Duluth. Jolly fought Golden Gloves in Minnesota, then won the NCAA Welterweight Title at the University of Wisconsin in 1942. "C'mon," he said after introductions. "Got a room for you at the YMCA. Get a good night's sleep and I'll pick you up in the morning."

The room at the "Y" was small, with a radiator that clanked all night. It only had one long, narrow window placed so high on the wall it was difficult to look out. I felt like I was in jail and wondered what I had gotten myself into.

The next morning Jolly picked me up, bought me breakfast, and took me to The Wisconsin State Journal where he worked as a reporter. He introduced me to everyone by saying, "I want you to meet a friend of mine, Bobby Morgan. He's going to be the next NCAA

Welterweight Champion." When we were out of range of the person I'd just met, I'd say "Jolly, I appreciated your saying that, but you don't even know me." He said, "I know Gerber, and he says you're going to do it." Then we'd be off to the next introduction where he'd say it again. What I didn't realize until later was that Jolly and Gerber were trying to give me the confidence that a good fighter needs, even if I had to borrow theirs.

When he introduced me that way to Louise Marston, Society Editor of the Journal, she wasn't too impressed at my boxing credentials. But after we talked a while, I could tell she liked me because she said, "Well, my boy, I think you need some work." I wasn't sure what she meant at first, but discovered as time went on that she was going to take me under her wing and smooth out what she saw as some very rough edges in my grammar and appearance.

Jolly then took me over to meet John Walsh, Coach of the Wisconsin Boxing Team and known as "The Winningest Coach in College Boxing." John Walsh, as an amateur boxer, set a record never to be equaled when he knocked out three opponents in an average of 90 seconds per opponent, all with a left hook, in his quest for the Northwest Golden Gloves Tournament title in 1935. His favorite expression, which I would hear often in the next several years was, "A left hook is a boy's best friend." What struck me about John Walsh was his kindness, a quality that stayed with him through the many decades that followed our first meeting in Madison.

I couldn't enroll in the September semester and had to wait for the February enrollment. John Walsh got me a job as a construction laborer and a rental room, both located only a few blocks from the University Field House where the boxing team trained. I was a construction laborer for eight hours, then worked out with the boxing team and ran three miles every night to get in my roadwork. After supper, I'd hang my work glove on a string from the ceiling and jab at it.

My roommate, a graduate student in Philosophy, didn't mind rooming with someone who boxed and worked on construction, but it drove him crazy when I jabbed at my work glove hanging from the ceiling while he was trying to study, which was most of the time. It also bothered him that I made gelatin and let it harden on the window ledge outside my room. But he earned his Ph.D. and I eventually made the team and we continued to talk to each other, even though we didn't have a lot to talk about.

My first year was a proving time, for grades and for boxing. And as far as girls, Gerber was right. They were a lot different than the ones in high school who wouldn't even talk to me.

I was in another world, far removed from Duluth, and didn't talk about home to anyone. But I stayed in close touch with Tom and Gram during the year and hitchhiked home for Christmas in 1951. Tom was two years from finishing high school, and that meant he'd be leaving Duluth too. We had a good Christmas. I loved seeing Gram again.

Uncle Ned was unusually quiet, so before I left I asked Tom about him. "He's still showing himself dirty movies and still nailing himself in his room once in a while. Oh, and he threatened to kill himself again by jumping in Lake Superior last January," Tom said. "Other than that, he's pretty normal, except ..."

"Except what?" I asked.

"Except that he's talking to the chickens like they were people."

"You're kidding!"

"No. He's even got names for some of them."

"Man, he's getting worse." I said.

"I don't know if he's worse or not. At least he doesn't want to kill the ones he's named. That's getting better in some ways, ain't it?" Tom asked.

"Yeah, in some ways. Sounds like he's softening up a little. But I'm still not going to tell people at school about him."

Waiting

"Vendors shouted as the fans streamed in, a babbling sound when the dressing room door opened, a muffled, foot shuffling buzz when the door closed, the sound of a crowd building, waiting."

Waiting

There was always a nerve-wracking "waiting" time before a fight. I didn't think much about waiting until I fought at the University of Wisconsin, where the caliber of opponents ratcheted up many degrees. Many of the college fighters had 40, 50, or more amateur fights in Golden Gloves, Diamond Gloves, AAU meets, or the military before getting to college. I had 24 fights as a member of the Duluth Golden Gloves team.

I waited a total of 27 times to fight at Wisconsin, usually against opponents I didn't know, opponents I wanted to hit harder and more often than they hit me, and knock out if possible, knowing they were in the ring to do the same to me.

In college, I was a natural welterweight at 147 pounds, and never had trouble making the weight. But the routine was the same for all of us — no food or drink until after the weigh-in at 11 a.m. Both teams weighed in at the same time in the same room. After the weigh-in, each team would go their own way for a big meal with teammates, a final relaxing, joking time. Then we'd split into smaller groups for a walk on campus before going to our rooms for a nap. Until then, I thought naps were for old people, but I slept every time.

After the nap, time played games — stretching, compressing, whispering to me, "The fight will take place. There will be no hurricanes, typhoons, or earthquakes to stop it. Your opponent will not have a heart attack or stroke. He will not suddenly fly to Brazil. He'll be there."

The afternoon dragged itself along to phone booths, newspaper stands, solitary walks, even to the dressing room where it disappeared, replaced by the final 90 minutes before the fights started. In those 90 minutes, I'd get my hands taped, put my robe on, lie on the bench, get up, take a leak, put the towel over my head, get up again, throw warm-up punches at the air, at the mirror, at the image of my opponent — to get rid of nerves, energy, and time.

Vendors shouted as the fans streamed in, a babbling sound when the dressing room door opened, a muffled, foot shuffling buzz when the door closed, the sound of a crowd building, waiting.

Each team had its own opening ceremony. At Wisconsin, the opening ceremony was both impressive and moving. The fighters from both teams entered the ring and stood on opposite sides while the flag was lowered from the blackness of the high ceiling of the

University Field House and the crowd sang The Star Spangled Banner. Then, back to the dressing room.

"Good Luck, Tommy," I said, patting our flyweight on the shoulder as he left for his fight. It might be ten or twelve minutes before Tommy would be back in the dressing room again, unless someone got knocked out. Time was winding down.

Always sooner than I expected, our trainer would say, "Come on, Morgan, let's go." He would usher me down the aisle, through the rows of fans saying, "Atta boy, Bobby," "Go get 'em," as I moved to those same four ring steps that seemed steeper now, then to the solidness of the canvas apron outside the ropes. I'd bend and step through the second strand of the ropes the trainer parted for me, hoping to God I didn't stumble and fall headlong into the ring. "Graceful, make it smooth and graceful, like I've done it a hundred times." I'd say to myself.

I'd move quickly to the center of the ring, where I'd pretend to listen to the referee's final instructions before returning to my corner to wait for the opening bell. As I walked back, time slowed again, to a sleepy pace, totally out of sync with my now changed feelings. I was eager now to hit this "nice enough guy" more often than he hit me, and try to knock him out before he knocked me out. So I would push that sleepy paced time faster, willing it to speed ahead, to that clanging bell, that loud, inevitable, clanging bell.

Sixty Seconds Of Glory

Andy Warhol said we would each receive our 15 minutes of fame. I cut that back to one minute for myself and called it "sixty seconds of glory." That was about the length of time the 13,000 boxing fans at the Wisconsin Field House roared their approval for my win in the finals of the NCAA Boxing Tournament in 1952. It assured Wisconsin the team title. It made me the NCAA Welterweight Champion.

My friend Jolly clipped the story from The Wisconsin State Journal in Madison and sent it to The Duluth News Tribune. They published the story there, too. It read, in part of the story quoting Jolly, "Morgan paced himself well in his championship tussle against the heavy-hitting LaForge. He was in just as good a condition at the finish as when he started. In his previous two bouts, Morgan indicated a tendency to tire perceptibly in the final round."

Jolly was kind in saying, "I indicated a tendency to tire perceptibly in the final round" because the truth was I barely survived the first two fights to get to the championship fight. I was tense and utterly exhausted by the end of those two fights. In the championship fight, I was hardly breathing hard. That probably was because I didn't follow Coach's instructions in the first two fights. I did it my way, and it was an exhausting scramble of tangled arms and getting hit too hard, too often. In the championship fight, it was as if I had purged myself of all the clumsiness and mistakes and was free now for that once in a lifetime performance.

It all happened so fast. The fight barely started and it was over. Then there was the spontaneous, thunderous roar from the crowd. I couldn't absorb all the feelings that flowed through me, but it seemed a chance for the Wisconsin boxing fans to come together for 60 seconds of feeling good, a release from the tension of the fight, a continuation of "the flow" that was the fight that night. It was sixty seconds of later-in-life daydreams, of joyous freedom and redemption for the badly fought and barely won fights of the previous two nights. It was a depth of feeling I would only know in quieter times years later—the moment I first told my wife Susan I loved her; the time alone in Northern Minnesota when I heard wolves howl somewhere far off; the final goodbye to my dying brother; the haunting flashes of memory when I was three years old and imagined I knew my mother, smelled her hair, felt her touch before she died.

It all ended too soon, maybe sixty seconds, maybe

only 30 or 45 seconds. However many there were, they lasted a long, long time and warm me yet, decades later.

A New Job, Another Christmas

Between serving my military obligation, which started a few months after graduation, and beginning a career, I took a job with a Chamber of Commerce in a small town. One of my first duties was to bring Santa Claus to town. We had a committee, but it was basically my job.

I decided to go for a Santa Claus package that was unique. Santa would enter town at precisely 4:30 p.m. with a motorized, glass enclosed sleigh, showing off eight reindeer. Santa would drive through downtown, waving to the children, throwing out candy canes, and bellowing, "Ho Ho Ho!" It was going to be terrific. The route would be lined with hundreds, maybe thousands of children and their parents.

The day arrived with full page ads and a feature story in the local paper. A sound truck circling the parade route announced Santa's imminent arrival. It was working. Children and parents were lining the curbs. Some children were holding on to their parents, some were on their parents' shoulders, others were being held in their parents' arms. It was beautiful. Everyone was waiting for Santa.

But 4:30 came and went. The sound truck driver kept circling the route saying, "Santa will be here. Don't worry kiddies." By 5:30, some of the parents were drifting home, dragging crying children. By 6:00 p.m., I had visions of being lynched.

Finally, Santa came. He had been in an accident. Worse than that, he was now drunk and weaving down the street in his sleigh. One of his reindeer had been "killed" in the accident, but it was hard to tell because the lights were out in the glassed-in portion of the sleigh.

The few parents who remained downtown were surly now. The darkened sleigh and the obviously drunken Santa weren't quite what they expected.

I was devastated. It was the long brown socks all over again.

Like Father, Like Sons?

"Benny met and married Arlene in Madison, and she provided some stability to his life again. They moved to Duluth in 1959. Tom was invited by his probation officer to 'leave Madison and never return, or you'll be arrested on the spot.' I was married and working in Chicago, so by 1959 all the Morgan brothers had left Madison."

Like Father, Like Sons?

Our dad was an alcoholic before the word was coined. None of us brothers wanted to be like our dad, yet we all seemed to be on the same path. Except for two things. Dad left us. And he hit our mom. Our unwritten code of conduct wouldn't allow us to do either. Yet, we did many of the other things Dad did, almost all of them alcohol related.

I had a good start to a good life. I had graduated from the University of Wisconsin, had been inducted into two honorary societies, and had been a member of the boxing team for three years. In my third year at school, I had married Barbara, the prettiest coed I could find. We had a 10 month old daughter, Kelly, and another child on the way. By graduation, I felt trapped. I started to "run away," not physically, but through the magic of Beefeater Gin martinis. I couldn't afford Beefeaters, but, after the first one always thought, "I deserve it. Look at the mess someone got me into."

Tom left Duluth in 1954, "The minute the ink was

dry on my high school diploma," was the way he put it, and came to Madison. Shortly after he arrived, he met and married a young lady named Jean, "Because she had big breasts and $16,000, my definition of 'true love' in those days," he said.

Starting in high school, Tom drank anything that gave him the same ride Beefeater martinis gave me. Tom's definition of an alcoholic was "anyone who drank with me more than once." Usually his drinking partners, following the first episode, would wake up after a long night of drinking, find themselves with a black eye, bruised knuckles or some other evidence of a bar fight and say, "Wow that was some experience! I'm never going to do that again." And most didn't.

During those years, Benny, who also married at 20, was living in Duluth, working at the steel plant, and rearing four children. In June of 1957, some inner voice told him to rush home from his late shift at the steel plant. He found his wife, Marion, his high school sweetheart, dead on the kitchen floor. She was 32. The death certificate said, "probable massive CVA," a heart attack. Benny, our tough brother who had seen death close up during the war, fell apart. He quit the steel plant, took his family to Madison, moved in with Tom and Jean temporarily, got a job, rented a home, and he and Tom started a two year binge of drinking and fighting in bars. Benny said to Tom after one of their drinking bouts, "The only way we're going to stop drinking is if we go out in the woods and tie ourselves to a tree."

Tom was still married and working as a real estate salesman in Madison. But he divorced in 1959 and, as Tom put it, "The dam broke. I never told my boss I was leaving and never contacted him during a nine day drunk that covered four states. I wrecked one car, lost another, ran out of drinking partners, lost 25 pounds, hadn't shaved or showered in days, and walked into the office in my dirty clothes. My boss didn't even recognize me until I asked him if there were any messages. Then he said one word, 'Out!'"

Benny met and married Arlene in Madison, and she provided some stability to his life again. They moved to Duluth in 1959. Tom was invited by his probation officer to "leave Madison and never return, or you'll be arrested on the spot." I was married and working in Chicago, so by 1959 all the Morgan brothers had left Madison.

Tom met and married a lovely woman named Donna and worked as a salesman for a Duluth radio station. They lived not far from Benny and Arlene in the west end of Duluth. Benny and Arlene were settling down, working hard and saving money so they could move farther north in Minnesota, perhaps to one of the towns along the Lake Superior shore. Benny wanted to be close to hunting and fishing, his lifelong passion. Both Tom and Benny had cut back on their drinking.

I was living in Chicago with my family and

realizing some things I never thought of in college. It wasn't Barb's fault, but I was beginning to regret being married so young. And with that regret came more drinking, more often, yet I felt it was still under control.

Tom, Benny, and I were now beginning to think the same thing. Our own drinking was under control, but one or both of our brothers were drinking way more than they should. And maybe, just maybe, we thought, one or both of our brothers might be, and we all hated to use the word, alcoholic.

The Funeral

"Gram had a resting place in Calvary Cemetery in Rice Township outside of Duluth, the same cemetery where our mom was buried. Gram would have been happy with that, to be with Mom."

The Funeral

I received a phone call that Gram was dying. It was 1963, and I was busy raising a family in the Chicago area 600 miles from Duluth. I had two daughters, Kelly nine, Kerry seven, and a son, Michael, two. Barbara and I were still together and we loved each other, but just weren't getting along.

The phone call, the first of two, came from Benny. He told me to stand by. He said he and Tom were with Gram and would stay with her until the end.

Gram didn't believe in doctors and healed most of our childhood sicknesses without one. Everything but a broken bone had a home remedy with Gram. She became doctor, nurse, and enforcer, making sure we took cod liver oil, her cure-all, her drug of choice. This woman who raised her own nine children, kept the five of us together after Mom died, helped raise a neighbor's child and two of our cousins, was now dying.

She had kept us safe from Uncle Ned's rage in those days when he was physically dangerous and she made it work with a garden and a chicken coop, very little money, and love hidden behind wet dishrags and moralistic poems. Gram never told us she loved us, but she lived by one of her sayings: "Actions speak louder than words."

The second call came a couple of hours later. "She died peacefully," Benny said.

"I'm glad for that. Was anyone else there?"

"Just me and Tom. I tried to get Chuck to visit," he said. "I found him sitting on a bar stool at The Green Parrot. When I walked in, he looked at me like I was the last person in the world he wanted to see. He said he knew why I was there."

I could visualize Benny, raising his left hand for emphasis. He always did that when he was agitated.

Benny went on, "I said to him, 'Chuck, if you want to see your Ma alive one more time, you better come with me. I'll give you a lift.'"

"What did he say?" I asked.

"He said, 'I can't go up there.'" Benny went on, "I raised my voice and said, 'Why not? Your mother's dying, for Christ sake!' He said, 'I can't go up dressed like this.' I told him, 'Look, It doesn't matter.' Then he told me, 'Okay. I'll be up in a little while.' I was so disgusted, I just left," Benny said.

"So, he never made it?"

"No." Benny added, "He's been drunk since he was captured at the Battle of the Bulge."

"Great excuse for drinking the rest of your life," I said.

"Yeah. When you coming up?"

"I'll be there for the funeral — earlier if I can get time off. Kelly wants to come. I'm going to see if I can take her out of school," I said.

Gram was 91 and couldn't keep going in that old house. She had broken the other hip and gangrene had set in earlier that year. Still, she pushed herself in the wheelchair over the basement trap door to the cupboards and sink, making meals for Uncle Ned and herself. Gram used to say, "Hard work never killed anyone." I never dared tell her she was wrong, but I thought she was wrong this time. It was easy to disagree now that I was six hundred miles away, 31 years old, and knew she couldn't hit me with that wet dishrag.

We were able to get Kelly out of school, so she came with me for the drive to Duluth.

Kelly hadn't met many of my relatives. She knew my brothers and my sister, Lu, from an earlier trip, but no one else.

The funeral was at Cathedral and, to my surprise, Monsignor Lynch said Mass. I always thought he only presided at funerals for important people in the parish, but there he was. I watched the altar boys stand where Tom and I used to stand. They were as somber as if it were their own grandmother in the casket.

So Gram was getting a good send off. Monsignor

Lynch was saying Mass and many of the people in the church were those Gram had touched at some time in her long life, Even Uncle Chuck was there, although he wouldn't attend the reception later at Uncle Hank's house because The Green Parrot was calling.

Gram had a resting place in Calvary Cemetery in Rice Township outside of Duluth, the same cemetery where our mom was buried. Gram would have been happy with that, to be with Mom.

My mind drifted from the casket to that old house and chicken coop, to the garden where Gram made us do our chores before we could play baseball, and different scenes floated through my head during the long service. "Gram, I can't turn over those rocks in the garden, they're too big, too..." I couldn't finish. Gram started reciting the poem, "Cannot, Edward, did you say ?" for the 500th time. "Drive those lazy thoughts away. Take the book from off the shelf. Don't be lazy, help your-self." I'd say, "But Gram, my name isn't Edward." It never mattered. She went on with the poem that never seemed to end. "Okay, okay, okay," I'd say and go back to turning over the dirt and rocks, which was a lot easier than listening to that poem again. I thought it was motivation of the worst sort when I was ten years old and had lots of other stuff to do. But it worked.

I knew Gram would always be my "Jiminy Cricket," my conscience forever perched on my shoul-der whispering in my ear, wagging her arthritic finger,

and repeating her poems as the situation demanded.
"Oh, I will not smoke tobacco ...." "Lips that touch
liquor shall never touch mine ...." And "Cannot, Edward," just to mention a few. I knew then and would
always know that the lesson of lessons from Gram was,
"Don't run away. Don't be like your dad." So my father
taught me the greatest lesson. By running away, he
taught me not to run away. Yet I might not have gotten
that message, except for Gram.

Dad never had a chance to defend himself. He
died of cancer in Seattle a couple of years before Gram.
And I never really knew his story. A long time ago, I
asked Gram, "There had to be more to it, didn't there,
Gram? Someone doesn't just run away, do they? I mean,
he must have had some good qualities, didn't he Gram?"
She wouldn't answer. "Gram?" I'd ask again. "He was
just a dirty, no-good, Irish rotter," she'd say. "But he was
a good fighter, wasn't he? I heard he used to go in a bar
and say, 'I can beat any Swede in the place.' And that he
could run up a barroom wall almost to the ceiling before
he had to drop to the floor. Isn't that pretty good, Gram?"
"No, it isn't pretty good. He just ran away. Can't you
understand? He left the five of you. Let it be a lesson,"
she'd say, wagging a stubby, arthritis-bent finger in my
face. Gram's toughness, her gruff but loving ways,
penetrated into some part of me so that now, so many
years later, I hear her still, "Never run away."

The Reception

My daughter, Kelly, was nine. She had never met Gram, but knew all the stories. She was fine during the funeral Mass, but as they placed Gram in the ground, she sobbed uncontrollably. I hugged her close.

We drove to Hank and Helen's house for the reception. Hank took me and Tom to Duluth Dukes baseball games, cut our hair until I got to high school, was at every one of my Golden Gloves fights, and kept us overnight when we had to get out of the house because of Uncle Ned's rages. So it was appropriate that he and his wife, Little Helen, would host the funeral reception. Tom and I had nicknamed her Little Helen so we could keep her straight from Big Helen, the one Gram always accused of stealing the mail. Hank and Little Helen had lived in the same house ever since we could remember. It was clean and well kept. The food for the reception was served on their Formica kitchen table and a couple of card tables.

Uncle Ned was standing by the kitchen table,

though he wasn't eating. Kelly wanted to meet this uncle she had heard so many stories about, so we walked over and I introduced her. She shook hands and didn't recoil at his missing finger, rough skin, and disheveled appearance. He still had on his mid-length overcoat, and later I found out why. "I'm glad to meet you, Uncle Ned. My dad's told me a lot about you," Kelly said. I had, and it was all bizarre, but Kelly was polite. Uncle Ned, this giant of a man who terrorized and confused us as little kids with his alcoholic fits of rage and self-pity, must have shrunk. He was skinny and stooped and looked frail. I couldn't believe it.

He said to Kelly, waving his hand in slow motion, "I ... I can't ... I can't understand if you talk fast." Kelly said it again, slower this time. He held out his hand again, as if the last time was a rehearsal. Kelly took it and looked into his face, this one-eyed face I had hated through the years, and said, very slowly, "I'm glad to meet you, Uncle Ned." She paused a long time. "My dad," and she paused again and pointed at me with her other hand, "told me a lot about you." Uncle Ned smiled as if it were a grand thing, the best compliment he'd ever received, and he wouldn't let go of Kelly's hand. After he met Kelly, he went out on the porch and took a swig from a pint whiskey bottle he had in his overcoat. Kelly said later she had never seen that, except in a movie.

That was it. The meeting Kelly still talks about. The extended handshake, the repeated phrase, and my obvious mixed feelings of anger and pity for this shrunken old man.

Later that night, as we were set to leave, Uncle Ned came over and said, "I don't know ..." He was talking even slower now. "I don't know what I'll do without Ma." He said it as if he were a six-year old. "Yeah, I know, Ned." I didn't know what else to say. There was a long, uncomfortable silence.

Then he said something I never expected and it turned out to be the real reason he wanted to talk again. "I got a lady friend. Gram never knew about her," he said, more drunk now, but more animated as he talked about her. I figured this lady friend must be a real beaut, but said I was glad. Then he started another sentence, hunting down every syllable. "My lady friend won't believe ... I ... I ... got a nephew that ... that was a champion boxer. Can you send me some ...," and he searched hard for the next word, "clippings?" I said, "Yeah, I will." He kept looking at me as though he didn't hear, and I said again, "Yeah, I promise, but we've got to go now." He didn't understand, so I motioned to the door while he lingered in his slow motion world.

I sent the clippings and a short letter. I told him to take care of himself and that I was glad he had a lady friend. And I added a phrase I never thought I'd say, "Thanks for helping to support us when we were kids." It killed me to say that, but I figured he could show his lady friend.

As I reflected on growing up in that old house, I did remember times when Uncle Ned drove Gram and us for a picnic or fireworks display and every so often to Mom's grave. Always times when he wasn't drunk. And I thought about Uncle Hank, what a decent guy he was, always making excuses for his brother. So if those two were brothers, maybe Uncle Ned could have been okay if he hadn't drunk so much. A small concession.

Kelly didn't know it, but her meeting Uncle Ned was helping me in my first step down a long and grudging, detour-filled road to forgiveness.

A Sometimes Holy Place

"We walked the squirrels' path and didn't get lost, and I felt pretty good about myself — from Michigan Avenue in Chicago one day to a squirrels' path in Northern Minnesota the next".

A Sometimes Holy Place

In the summer of 1968, Benny and Arlene finally made the move they had worked and saved for since they left Madison nine years earlier. They found a small home with two acres on the shores of Lake Superior, 80 miles North of Duluth, 85 miles South of Canada. A people-free place, but not enough for Benny who wrote shortly after he settled in, "I passed two cars on my way to work this morning. I think I'm going to move to some place more isolated."

Benny could walk out of his kitchen into the massive Superior/Quetico National Forest, the preserved land of woods and waters that extended all the way into Canada. And he walked those woods every day before and after work, regardless of the weather. He and Arlene also camped and fished every weekend. Benny had never read Thoreau, but he was "marching to a different drummer" as Thoreau had done 125 years earlier, and he sounded happier now than he had ever been. He loved Northern Minnesota the way I loved Chicago. He had found his Shangri La.

Benny wanted to share it with me, but I was hooked on career climbing in the big city life of Chicago and hiking in the woods or fishing on some hard-to-get-to-lake didn't fit in with my ambitions. Benny also wanted to share it with Tom, but neither of us had heard from Tom for a couple of years, though we thought he was in California.

Soon after he was settled in, he called and tried to get me to visit. "Come on up," he said. "We'll go fishing in Swan Lake. It's a three portage trip, but at the end of the last portage we'll reach a six foot wide stream that bends and winds for about two miles and leads directly into Swan Lake." He painted a tranquil scene. "We can drink from the stream — and once in a while a loon will swim underwater past us. You know, a person can go a lifetime and never see a loon up close. And in Swan Lake you won't meet another fisherman."

I wasn't sure I wanted any of that. Go from Michigan Avenue to loons in Swan Lake? But later that summer, both my job and failing marriage were getting to me, so I called Benny late one night. "I've got to get away for awhile," I said. "Can I come up?"

"Get in the car and come up tonight." he said. I was on my way before I thought about it and arrived before he had to go to work the next day. He drew me a map of the woods behind his house and told me to take a walk. "You'll enjoy it. It'll take a half day." he said.

It started as a wide path that crossed a creek, then narrowed to what Ben called "a squirrels' path."

"If you think you can't see the path, look ahead of you ten or fifteen yards and you'll see its outline. Don't look down where you're standing or you won't see it. After you pass the creek you'll find an abandoned shack where I used to stick dynamite caps between the loose boards and explode 'em with a 22. Take Jiggs along for company. You can't get lost if Jiggs is with you," he said.

Jiggs, his small terrier, sniffed every inch of the trail. And when I took my boots off to let my feet hang in the creek, Jiggs took a big drink and stayed next to me. We found the shack. We walked the squirrels' path and didn't get lost, and I felt pretty good about myself — from Michigan Avenue in Chicago one day to a squirrels' path in Northern Minnesota the next.

We went to Swan Lake the next morning. It was three portages all right. Long ones, with Ben carrying the canoe and me carrying the back packs and canoe paddles. We paddled the small stream where the grasses weaved under water and it was as pretty as anything I'd ever seen. A loon didn't swim by on the way in, but we heard them call each other on Swan Lake and watched them dive and come up, always in a different spot than we expected.

My brother had a great ability to listen, and he didn't say much as I poured out my marriage and job problems. Then he told me to sit back and enjoy. I tried, and somehow the beautiful streams, the birds, the evergreens reflecting in the water among the lily pads, and the long grasses weaving in the clear waters under the canoe seemed to unburden me as we floated in the soothing silence of Swan Lake. I never expected any of that. I was drawn back to Ben's Shangri La many more times, to fish in Swan Lake, to hunt with him, to join him in capturing smelt with buckets in the early spring as they ran up the stream entering Lake Superior just off his property, and sometimes to just sit with him in his boathouse and talk.

That visit with Benny at his small home on the shores of Lake Superior in 1968 turned out to be the first in a succession of firsts that would change the way I looked at life. It would be my first fishing trip to a wilderness lake, my first deer hunt, my first transcendent moment in nature when I knew that nature was a sometimes holy place.

Letters From Benny

"The snow is all but melted and the grass is starting to turn a nice Irish color. Wow! It's sure nice to be alive and healthy. I'm a millionaire, Bob."

Letters From Benny

Feb. 17, 1969

Dear Bob,

Some of the snow has melted, but it's still deep.

The deer are in very bad shape. They're being slaughtered on the highways, by wolves and dogs in the woods, and they're starving in the deep snow. We bought a couple bales of hay for the deer and spent most of the weekend cutting underbrush. We also used our snowmobiles to make new trails so the deer get a chance to run on them.

Last weekend Arlene and I went for a snowmobile ride. We found a poor doe lying dead, half eaten by a wolf. The noise of our machines must have scared off the wolf. It was a pitiful sight to see. She was practically eaten alive.

Hope to see you all soon. Ben, Arlene, and Jiggs.

Jan. 13, 1970

This is your big brother way up here in God's Country.

Wish you could have been here last night. It was just beautiful. There was a quarter moon and a million stars, all of them bright and reflecting off the big lake. They lit up the lake and our back yard and you could see the deer walking around feeding.

I walked out the front door so as not to disturb them. It was very calm. I could hear the wolves howling. They just made a kill.

It's just beautiful, Bob, and it makes me sad to think that some day, this will all be gone. I thank God that I lived in some of it, even if it is the tail end.

Feb. 6, 1970

...I broke another trail, so I've got about 15 to 20 miles of snowmobile trails in the boondocks now. Last Monday it was 40 below with a 30 mile wind. Wind chill was an even 100 below....

April 22, 1970

...I went for a little spin on the Honda this a.m. and saw many deer and also a big moose ahead of me. The moose ran into the gravel pit where you and Mike were snowmobiling. The snow is all but melted and the grass is starting to turn a nice Irish color. Wow! It's sure nice to be alive and healthy. I'm a millionaire, Bob.

...The big trout are starting to spawn and any day now the smelt will start to run. They'll be so thick in the Cascade River you'll be able to pick them up with your hands like we did last year. The water just churns and turns black with smelt. I wish you could make it up next Friday for the weekend. We could go smelting. They're delicious. I'll even smoke some for you.

Well folks, I have some bad news to tell you now. Last Good Friday at 11 a.m., Jiggs was killed instantly when he ran in front of a car. We really took it hard and we miss him very much. He was one of the family.

Hope you can make it up soon. Sounds like you have some real good fishing in Illinois. We might sell out and move down there. Let me know, Bob, what week you can come up so I can put in for my vacation. Ok, brother mine — hope to see you all soon.

May 18, 1970

...Arlene and I went fishing Saturday early a.m., opening day. We fished all day in a near blizzard. It was cold, snowing, and windy, just plain miserable. There's still snow in the woods and the water's just too damn cold. The fish didn't cooperate....

Nov. 3, 1970

...We visited Arlene's folks. Holy Christ, it was boring. The highlight came on Saturday night when we all watched some game show. Wish you were there! I could have had as much fun being dragged bare-assed across a cactus field by my balls during a wild pig stampede, in a blizzard, with a hangover....

Feb. 1, 1971

...Arlene and I tried out our new electric blanket twice. The first night the power went out and stayed out all night. Last night we tried it again. This blanket has two control dials on it, one for Arlene on her side and one for me on mine. She gets the control gizmos mixed up. She got too warm, so she turned hers down. All it did was turn my side down. I got cold, so I turned mine up, which made her side a lot hotter. She then turns hers off, which leaves me with nothing but a cold ass. I turn mine all the way up and she's sweating bullets....

March 2, 1971

...There's been a big-ass Bobcat hanging around the house lately. "Lady" is playing Russian Roulette every time she has to go outside to take a leak....

March 13, 1971

...Arlene's going to the beauty parlor for a checkup. I think she's long past due. The other morning she walked out in the back yard and all I saw was flying snow, flying hoofs, and deer running every which way. She not only scared the deer, but they were bringing back hay they'd stolen two years before.

Aug. 3, 1971

...Me and Arlene went into Swan Lake and saw a Timber Wolf chase a deer into the water. The deer swam right out to us in the canoe....

Aug. 17, 1971

...It's finally cooled off, back to the old air conditioned air again. It's been perfect over the weekend and today. It gets down in the low '40's at night. I suppose you're wondering if this is a letter or a friggen weather report....

* * *

There were many letters, phone calls, and visits between us dating from that first visit to Swan Lake. Tom came back to Illinois in 1971 and was able to spend some good times with Benny in the North Country, too. But the three of us brothers were drinking more heavily than ever.

The drinking didn't stop Tom and me from going into business together in 1974. We agreed on three rules for our business:

1. It would be a 50-50 partnership
2. We would never work on Sundays.
3. We'd always make time to see our brother in the North Country.

Don't Take Yourself Too Seriously

"When I got home I went to the liquor cabinet that was just inside the front door and drank some more. Mike talked about supper, but I wasn't hungry. I told him to go ahead and fix himself something. He did. We ate in silence. Mike went to his room. I sat at the kitchen table, drinking."

Don't Take Yourself Too Seriously

From three years old to age seventeen, I lived with Uncle Ned, who had one eye, nine fingers, a filthy mind that brought him to expose himself to my two older sisters, a personality that flip-flopped between irrational anger and self-pity, and an addiction to alcohol that eventually turned his brain to mush. He called our family stupid and worthless, and we hated him as we were growing up.

But, as the years went on, he would do such things as eat Van Camp Pork and Beans off a newspaper and wear his glass eye when it was broken in half, stuffing the broken half with cotton, apparently figuring no one would notice. The very thing he wanted us to do when we were growing up, to feel sorry for him when he got into his self-pitying moods and did things like sleeping in the chicken coop at 30° below, or trying to jump into Lake Superior when it was frozen solid, was now happening and he wasn't even aware of it.

So instead of beating him up when we were old

enough, a thought that gave us satisfaction and sustenance when we were growing up, we just let him be. We watched him deteriorate from alcohol, poor diet, and residual meanness. His self-consuming hatred, that high-octane fuel that kept him going, was running low. He was doing to himself what none of us would have dreamed of doing to him.

From about age 22 to 42, I drank, increasing the amount of alcohol until I was so miserable I had to stop or die prematurely. The alcohol brought out the meanness in me. I argued to prove people wrong, I flip-flopped in my moods, became irrational, selfish, self-centered, and Godless. I was becoming Uncle Ned with two eyes and ten fingers.

I'm told no one knows when they "cross the line" from social drinking to alcoholic drinking. I didn't know. It may have been when I started two and three martini lunches in Chicago and dreaded that long ride home on the "Burlington," where I was surrounded by businessmen in double-breasted suits who I knew were "leading lives of quiet desperation," as Thoreau described "the mass of men." Who wanted to be sober with that group?

Or when I wouldn't go to a restaurant that didn't serve cocktails, or go out with people who didn't drink like me, or when I started drinking every noon and kept at it until I went to bed that night, only to start over the next day.

Or when my martinis no longer needed a dash of vermouth. Or when I ran out of vodka or gin and drank that unused vermouth with maraschino cherry juice. Or when I started drinking scotch with warm milk because I didn't like scotch.

Or after Barb wrote me three long and thoughtful letters, each one stronger, trying to convince me I was an alcoholic and should do something about it. We were still living together, but letters were the only way we could keep a conversation going.

Or after Barb finally left in September of 1974, and my three children asked me to stop drinking "at least for the Christmas Holidays." I did, but felt it was one of the toughest things I'd ever done, and couldn't wait to start up again on January 1.

Or when I replaced God with self-pity and a line from a Neil Diamond song, "I've got an emptiness deep inside and I've tried, but it won't go away."

On March 21, 1975, I went to Rockford, Illinois, for a business lunch with Tom. I didn't go the quick and easy tollway route. I left early and went on Highway 20 where there were a lot of taverns. I wanted to get a head start on Tom, my drinking and business partner.

Mike, my 13 year old son, who had chosen to stay with me after the divorce, was home and could take care of himself after school, so I didn't have to be home at any certain time. I planned an afternoon of drinking with Tom, maybe into the evening as well, as happened so many other times.

When I saw Tom at the restaurant I was shocked at his appearance. He didn't have the deep, dark circles under his eyes and he wasn't jumpy and nervous and irritable as he often was before his first drink. Tom also had someone else at the table. Tom quietly explained that he hadn't had a drink for six weeks and had, in fact, joined AA. "Meet, Gail," Tom said. "He's my sponsor."

This was going to be a lot of fun, I could tell. Here's Tom, not drinking, looking happy, healthy, and relaxed, sitting with another happy looking guy who also happened to be his sponsor. I soon found out worse news. Gail was a tombstone salesman. My trip was shot, my afternoon was shot, maybe my life was shot. "What if this guy tries to get me into AA? It could screw up everything," I thought.

I ordered a martini and told the waitress not to bring me another one, even if I begged her. She promised. Naturally, I ordered another one and she didn't keep her promise. Whatever happened was going to be her fault. Neither Tom nor the Tombstone guy tried to stop me. They just sat there looking content. I was getting more and more irritated. We did talk a little business, but I couldn't wait to leave so I could drive home on Highway 20 and drink without guilt.

Before I left, Gail got in one parting shot. He said, "If I can help you in any way, don't hesitate to call." I figured that would be the day when I'd need help from a tombstone salesman. What the hell was wrong with my tough brother, not drinking any more and having this guy for a sponsor?

When I got home I went to the liquor cabinet that was just inside the front door and drank some more. Mike talked about supper, but I wasn't hungry. I told him to go ahead and fix himself something. He did. We ate in silence. Mike went to his room.

I sat at the kitchen table, drinking. I began to think about Tom getting sober and wondering, just wondering, if I might have a drinking problem. Barbara had been telling me that for a couple of years, and then wrote those three long letters, and finally backed it up by leaving and divorcing me the previous September.

As I sat at the table thinking about that, the phone rang. It was Gail. I wondered if this tombstone salesman was going to start bugging me. He's not satisfied getting Tom into AA, he's going to work on me, too. But for some reason, I was not only receptive, I was glad he called. He talked about not drinking and I listened. Before he hung up, he suggested I call Alcoholics Anonymous. "It's pretty late, Gail," I said. "They couldn't help me tonight anyway." He said, "No, just look in the yellow pages and give them a call. I think you'll be surprised." So I hung up and, before I could talk myself into waiting until tomorrow, when I knew I might put it off again, I called AA. A man answered and I told him I thought I needed help to quit drinking — one of my most understated understatements.

In about a half hour, two men came to the door. It was almost as if they were sitting somewhere waiting for my call. They both looked happy, too, and I thought I was going crazy. They came into my kitchen and started talking and acting like they had all the time in the world. One of them had a drinking pattern like mine. And he had an answer for all my objections. After a couple of hours one of the men had to leave, but the other man, named Jack, stayed a couple more hours. And before he left he said something that I thought was the wisest thing anyone had ever said to me. I said, "Jack, how can I go to bed without drinking? I've been drinking all day." He said, "Just don't take another drink until your head hits the pillow, and then tomorrow don't drink even if you have to work at it fifteen minutes at a time."

There it was, the Ten Commandments rolled into one sentence. He gave me his phone number and said he'd take me to an AA meeting tomorrow. I was stunned. Here I had no intention of stopping drinking when the day started and did everything to make sure I had plenty of liquor in me by nightfall. Yet I was now making plans to go to bed without another drink, and then asking someone how I could get through the next day without drinking. This time it wasn't a promise to my kids and I wasn't stopping because Barb was nagging me. I was stopping because something was happening to me. Some people who drank the way I did, who had the same kinds of problems I was having, were now sober and were willing to help me.

At my first AA meeting I met "hope." It was in those 20 or so men and women who looked as happy as Tom and Gail. They held a "First Step Meeting," which meant they each told their stories for my benefit. Some stories were worse than mine and a few weren't as bad. But each had reached the stage I had, where they knew they needed help. I had built this wall around myself, brick by brick. Not a spacious house, mind you, a tight fitting chimney more than a house. No one could squeeze in with me anymore, not even God, and I couldn't get out — until that first night at AA.

When I finally stopped drinking, I kept learning the same lesson, as if I had to have this lesson sink in for all time. It started in May of 1975, when I attended an AA conference in Starved Rock, Illinois. Each of the twelve speakers on stage was to speak for one minute on each of the 12 steps of AA. The last speaker was a spastic. I had only been sober two months and was still loaded with arrogance. I wondered what this man could possibly say that I didn't already know. He couldn't even control his arms. And his wife was also a spastic. This was going to be embarrassing.

But he was as eloquent as John Kennedy and told us how grateful he was to have found AA. If someone had put a pistol to my head, they couldn't have stopped my sobbing. The walls of arrogance didn't fall forever, but they were badly damaged by that beautiful human being. The fat people, the dirty and smelly people I didn't want to listen to or even sit near, always taught me lessons I didn't know I needed. This assault on my arrogance from the most unlikely and unexpected sources was gradually squeezing out the last vestiges of the Uncle Ned in me. I was learning to become a human being again from other human beings I once looked down on.

Goodbye, Geraldine

"Susan wasn't ready for me or anyone else. But in my eagerness, I pursued her with cards, letters, phone calls, flowers, poems, and lots of visits that almost drove her away."

Goodbye, Geraldine

My first love was Geraldine, who stayed at the communion rail when I made that mistake as an altar boy back in grade school. I was so shy I never told her I was in love with her, whatever that meant. She rarely talked to me after that episode, so it didn't matter anyway.

Through the years there were other "'Geraldines" but no one like Susan. I met her in 1977, two years after getting sober. Susan had been married to a practicing alcoholic for nine years before we met, so I had to do a lot of convincing. I proposed to Susan when I was the speaker at an AA meeting of about 200 people. I told them I prayed for someone I could love and grow old with about the time I was beginning to get sober and was beginning to know what love was, and wasn't. And here came Susan, the answer to a prayer. I put her on the spot that night, but I knew she was tough enough to say no.

From the first day we met, I knew I wanted to marry her. I had been single for two years and was ready. She had just left a stifling marriage where her ex-husband tried to run her life, even to the extent of telling her how to fold the toilet paper so it looked right hanging in the bathroom. Susan wasn't ready for me or anyone else. But in my eagerness, I pursued her with cards, letters, phone calls, flowers, poems, and lots of visits that almost drove her away.

In spite of her telling me not to rush her, I still couldn't understand why she was pulling away from me. So I turned to my brother, Tom, for advice. He said, "Treat her as if she were a rare china cup." It sounded like a good idea, so I naturally took it to the extreme. I went home and put a note on the phone, the refrigerator, the mirror in the bathroom, the bookshelf, and even on the door knob. All the notes said the same thing, "Don't call Susan." My avalanche of love notes, phone calls, and visits stopped, not slowed, stopped — dead. After a few days, each day seeming a year long, Susan called and said, "Keep the cards and letters coming."

The Last Hunt

"At home a week later, I dreamed I shot a deer in my living room. Blood was splattered on the walls, the curtains, the carpet, and all over me. I wondered how I'd ever clean up before my wife got home, so I frantically called a friend."

The Last Hunt

When Benny invited me on my first deer hunt along with his old hunting buddy, Dan Deutschaeffer, I wasn't even sure how to load the 30-30 rifle Dan loaned me. I was given a quick lesson about 4 o'clock that morning. Then Benny led me to a tree stand he had made for me earlier that fall. We made so much noise tromping through the woods getting to the stand I figured every deer within miles heard us.

"I'm going to make a wide circle and see if I can drive anything toward you," Benny whispered. The whispering seemed wasted as he moved away to more loud leaf crunching and twig breaking, but time and distance swallowed his footsteps and soon it was still.

As I sat in the emerging daylight, I heard ravens cawing in the distance, then the "whoosh, whoosh" sound of their wings as they flew directly overhead, then gathering silence as they flew on.

I thought I heard wolves howl after the ravens passed, but couldn't be sure, so I held my breath and listened. Then I heard it, a distant wolf pack, their howling floating through the ravens' wake, a wild, chilling sound that stopped, then started, then stopped again, the last distant howl still with me.

The season would start as soon as light allowed hunters to see clearly before shooting. I watched two squirrels chase each other through the dry leaves then up and around a nearby tree as I settled in for what I thought would be a long wait.

Within minutes, I heard dry leaves rustling in the distance, the sound moving lightly towards me. I thought, "it's a herd of squirrels." I knew squirrels didn't move in herds, but my rational mind stopped working when I heard it because the other part of me knew it was a deer, and I wondered if I was ready for it.

An eight point buck came directly down the path in front of my stand and I shot and killed it. I couldn't believe it. I finished my first hunt the first 15 minutes of opening day.

Benny came back and said over and over again, "I'm more happy for you than if I got it myself," as we field dressed the deer and dragged it back to his house on the lake.

Dan came back at noon. Before he came in, Benny said, "Watch this." Dan saw the deer and looked surprised. "Who got the deer?" Dan asked. "Bob did, in the first 15 minutes," Benny said. "You bastard!" he yelled at me." You lucky bastard. Hey, Ben, I want you to know your brother is a lucky bastard."

I was never that lucky again, even though Benny and I hunted together almost every year after that. I changed my definition of luck as the years went on. It wasn't in killing the deer. My luck, my good fortune, was in being with Benny on all those hunts. And I never thought it would end. The 1990 deer season was the last time Benny and I hunted together. He had been diagnosed with cancer of the colon more than a year earlier and had been given two years to live.

On that day, Benny and I were hunting separate areas when I saw a buck walk the opening between two evergreen trees. It was an easy shot and I was sure I hit it as it disappeared behind one of the evergreens. I put the safety on my rifle and ran noisily to where I thought it would be. If it was suffering, I wanted to finish it off. The deer was there, but I had missed it completely. He was standing about 10 or 12 feet away, curious, beautiful, looking directly at me. The deer didn't move as I raised my rifle and aimed for its chest. I shot and killed it. And felt like throwing up.

At home a week later, I dreamed I shot a deer in my living room. Blood was splattered on the walls, the curtains, the carpet, and all over me. I wondered how I'd ever clean up before my wife got home, so I frantically called a friend. "Harry, come over. Hurry. I killed a deer in my living room and it's a mess." Harry wasn't at all surprised. "I'll be right over," he said. Then I woke up.

That dream did it. I never wanted to kill another deer or any other living creature as long as I lived. Yet I really didn't want Benny to know. I thought, "If he had longer to live ..." — and stopped. It was the first time I had allowed the thought of his dying to enter my consciousness. "If he had longer to live, I'd have told him. I can't tell him now." I finished the thought and let it seep in.

On October 28, 1991, I made another of the many calls that both Tom and I made to see how Ben was feeling. Arlene answered and said he was in bed already. "He only eats because he has to, and he's sleeping a lot during the day. He's getting weaker and hasn't even gone out in the back yard the past few days. Yet, he thinks he can make it out in the woods again if you come up. The season starts November 8th." she said.

"Absolutely, tell him I'll be there," I said. I called the next morning about 9:30. Ben answered and sounded great. I felt I could joke with him again so I said, "I wasted a phone call last night. I didn't expect you'd be in bed so early."

He picked up on his buddy Dan's favorite saying, "You bastard," and we were off, laughing and making plans for the deer season that would start in ten days.

On November 7, I walked into Benny's house and, after greetings, asked how he felt. "Do you want the truth, or do you want to hear a whopper and have me tell you I feel good?" he asked with a weak smile. He was in his robe and would stay in it during my visit except for one brief trip to the garage.

We talked about a lot of things that day, but not about the deer season that was starting tomorrow. He spoke of his love for Mitzi, his small dog who followed him constantly. "When I sleep in the afternoon, Mitzi sleeps with me. When I get up in the middle of the night, Mitzi's right there. When I'm in the Lazy Boy she lays in my lap or at my feet always looking at me except when I read the paper, then she turns and faces my feet." He chuckled a little as he said it.

Then he talked about tomorrow. "It's the first opening day of deer season I've missed in 45 years," he says. "I'm sorry, Bob." I could see the pain and fatigue in his eyes and told him, "You don't ever have to apologize to me for anything." He suggested I walk the property that afternoon and look for deer signs and he gave me some tips on where to look.

The next morning, I left with my rifle and told Ben I'd see him later in the day. I hadn't walked 25 yards from his back door into the woods when I saw two deer and stopped immediately. They saw me, but couldn't make out who or what I was. The wind was blowing towards me, so they couldn't pick up my scent. We stared at each other for one or two minutes as they twisted and cocked their heads to try to figure out what they were looking at.

They moved from under the big evergreen where one of them had been bedded down and both stood broadside to me. I raised my rifle and sighted in on one of them, but gradually lowered my rifle. I couldn't shoot. One of the deer moved toward me until it caught my scent, then snorted, alerting the other deer, and they turned and bounded out of sight.

I stayed in the woods until noon. When I entered the house, Benny was up. "Did you see anything?" he asked. "Yes, two deer, but they were out of range." It was the first and only time I ever lied to Benny.

I stayed a few more days. All the while he had a flu-like sickness, was weak, and had trouble moving about. He had mini blackouts, his stomach was terribly bloated, and he didn't feel like eating. He had discontinued the experimental pills from the Mayo Clinic because they made him so sick. Chemotherapy had been over for a couple of months.

"The cancer's growing in my gall bladder now, and there's nothing they can do about it." he said. I didn't know what to say. At supper he couldn't eat and finally broke down and left the table, apologizing. Arlene helped him into the Lazy Boy and returned to the kitchen.

"It's going to get worse," she said, and cried. It was the first time I had seen her cry, but she wouldn't let Benny see her. I went to Ben again. "Don't worry about crying. You're the most courageous man I've ever known," I told him. The release of tension helped him and for the first time he told me some of his wartime experiences, things Tom and I wanted to know when he first got home in 1945.

"I was in one shipwreck and several tropical storms," he said, "one with 175 mph winds on Okinawa. The bombers were on the ground facing into the wind with their engines gunned to keep them from blowing away. Black fighter planes were lashed to the ground and the sand stripped the paint so they were metallic in the morning." he said.

"I saw 250 American sailors killed by a Japanese kamikaze pilot who flew his plane down the ship's smokestack. The men were buried head to toe, wrapped in Army blankets," he said. "I had the last rites of the Church three different times from malaria and dysentery. The first time, because a nun saw the scapular around my neck, she stayed with me as much as possible, nursing me back to health. So, I'm not afraid to die," he said. "I'll miss all this." And he motioned to the outdoors. I knew what he meant.

"I was driving an Army tanker truck filled with hi-octane fuel when a Japanese plane came over strafing the area. I jumped out of the truck and, in the excitement, crawled under it." he said, and smiled a faint smile at the irony of it.

"I was in hundreds of air raids and once, after the Japanese Imperial Marines parachuted on our island, a buddy and I were lost in the jungle and could hear the Japanese all around us. We made a pact that we'd kill ourselves before we'd be captured," he said.

I slept a troubled sleep that night and heard Ben walking around about 3 a.m. I got up and joined him at the kitchen table. He was hungry for a change, so we shared a turkey sandwich and talked awhile. "Arlene wanted me to make it through the summer," he said. "Then she wanted me to make it though my birthday at the end of September." I know he's setting me up for a joke of some sort. "Then she said, 'Hang on until deer season.' Now she's saying, 'try to make it through Christmas.' I'm going to try," he said, "but if she asks me to make it to Easter, I'm going to tell her, the hell with it." And he manages another faint smile. "If I hang around too long I'm going to go out at the same weight I came in — seven pounds." He felt better. Mitzi was in the kitchen and followed Benny back to bed.

The next day Benny got dressed for the first time and showed me some equipment in the garage, but he almost blacked out. I opened the door for him and he saw Mitzi chase a mole that had been hiding in the shed. The mole ran along the shoveled path with Mitzi in pursuit, but Ben called Mitzi off. "I can't hurt anything any-more," he said. "That little thing is helpless, but it makes a stand every so often against Mitzi. It doesn't seem fair," he said.

The season was over. We had a lot of good talks. It was time for me to go home again. As I was leaving, the mole scurried back down the shoveled path towards the shed. I left the back door open long enough for him to get in, and he disappeared under the bench.

Two months later, on January 17th, Tom called. "Ben died late last night," Tom said. "He's blazed another trail for us."

QUICK SERVICE   LOW RATES

Form 1300C

WESTERN UNION
MONEY ORDER MESSAGE

Money by Telegraph and Cable to All the World

A. N. WILLIAMS
PRESIDENT

NEWCOMB CARLTON
CHAIRMAN OF THE BOARD

C. WILLEVER
FIRST VICE-PRESIDENT

No. A19

19 43 19

To MRS BARBARA MORGAN BELSCH
MR., MRS. OR MISS

414 9 AVE WEST
ADDRESS

TRANSIT TIME OF THIS
MONEY ORDER
MINUTES

The Money Order paid you herewith HARRY J. MORGAN
NAME

at SEATTLE WASH
PLACE
included the following message:

MORE MONEY SOON LOVE

THE WESTERN UNION TELEGRAPH COMPANY

Dad — In Shades Of Gray

My images of my dad are formed from black and white photographs and from telegrams saying, "Will send money soon. Regards, Harry." Those things I can touch and get hold of. But there were no letters, nothing else in writing. Everything else was second hand, except for that visit from Dad when I was 16.

My sister, Al, was 10 when Mom died. Al tried to defend Dad from Gram's onslaughts, but that's hard to do when you're 10 and you have a tough lady like Gram coming at you, blaming your father for causing the death of her beloved daughter, and then running away. So that battle outcome was predetermined. But Al met our dad in Seattle before he died, and she liked him. "He had a good sense of humor, and he did send money for us, but Gram never let on that he did," she said. "And he wasn't drinking anymore," she added as an afterthought.

"Gram said Mom had a black eye from him when she was in the coffin," I argued.

"That wasn't true," Al said.

"And Aunt Nita said that he showed up at the funeral with his two front teeth missing from a bar fight. She can't talk about him at all without calling him 'that jackass.'"

"That's not true, either," Al said.

"Al, when I called Aunt Nita to get some information, she got angry just talking about him, like it happened yesterday instead of almost six decades ago. I thought Nita was going to have a stroke."

"Nita and Mom were very close," Al said, justifying Nita's strong feelings after all those years. "But she and Gram hated him and he couldn't do anything right once he left."

Benny was 13 when Mom died. He didn't have a lot of good things to say about Dad. "He was tough," Benny said, "I'll give him that. But he didn't treat Mom well at all. I got the hell beat out of me whenever I tried to defend Mom against him." I never thought to ask Benny about Mom's black eye in the coffin or Dad's missing two front teeth at the funeral.

Whenever I asked Al or Benny or Nita about our dad, I didn't ask a lot of questions. I would say, "Tell me about our dad," and leave it open for what they wanted to say. Oh, I asked a few questions, but none that got to the heart of who he was, or none that tried to change their already set view of him.

I still can't feel anger. And I wonder why. He's not a hero to me, but he's not a bum either. Maybe it was his toughness I admire. And maybe I make excuses for him about leaving because of his apparent alcoholism, although the term in those days was, "He was a drunk."

I know what it is to drink and not be able to stop. And drink and do things you wouldn't do when sober. And I know that drinking is the classic form of running away from your problems. I know all that. Yet I wonder if I will ever know enough about him to get out of "neutral" whenever I think of him.

Other men became my heroes. Benny was my first hero, and became more of a hero as we both grew older. My boxing trainer, Bob Gerber, was a hero to me when I first got to know him at 14 years old, and he remains a hero and close friend. Father Lutz, a Catholic priest and dear friend who helped me get sober, and taught me to love again, will always be my hero. My brother Tom, is a big hero and one I can talk to every day. How many heroes can you talk to every day? But no one ever takes the place of a mother or father. I know because I searched the streets of Duluth and listened for their voices in the early morning foghorns and tried to feel that way about Gram in her most tender moments. But no one came close.

And one day I stopped looking.

Chocolate

My addictions didn't just disappear when I got into AA. Chocolate chip cookies have taken the place of alcohol. You can have your martini, I'll take cookies. No one ever went to jail for eating cookies, or had car accidents, or beat their wives, or went insane, or died. So it's not so bad. My dentist loves it.

Susan, who has never seen me drunk, doesn't bake anymore. And that's good. I used to lick out the bowl, eat a few cookies when they were just dough drops on the cookie sheet, a few more when they were served, and even more when they were cooked and wrapped in tinfoil in the freezer, waiting for a special occasion.

Susan stopped baking one day when, in the early days of our marriage, I returned from work and found about 64 small chocolate chip cookies. I ate one, then two, then about twenty before she stopped me. "You'll never eat supper," she said.

So I proved her wrong. I ate the spaghetti supper, watched TV on a waterbed, then found myself in the bathroom about 1:00 a.m., sicker than most hangovers, berating Susan. "Don't ever, ever bake chocolate chip cookies again," I said. "I'll never touch another one. Never."

The next morning I got up and ate the rest of them. All of them.

I'm older now, still trying to grow up. It's not easy. My brother Tom put it best, "It wasn't a happy child-hood," he said, "but it's been a long one."

Who Ate My Brownie?

"There was a spot in Wisconsin, about two hours from us, that had the best brownies in the State — delicious, thick, chocolate frosting brownies. I eagerly drove without a break, got gas, bought two brownies, ate one quickly to get my chocolate fix, then left the other one in the bag and put it on the dash of our truck while I went to browse through an antique store. As I approached the truck after shopping, I remembered the brownie in the bag on the dash board. It wasn't there."

Who Ate My Brownie?

It's pretty bad when I have to admit I learn more from my dogs than they learn from me. It's not supposed to work that way. And between our two dogs Chelsea and Cozette, the better teacher is Chelsea. She's the bigger of the two, the leader of the pack. Part Labrador, and part lots of other breeds.

Susan and Chelsea met when Susan went to Noah's Ark, an animal shelter in Rockford 11 years ago to buy cat food. As Susan was about to leave, a large, black dog was brought in by a woman who found it wandering the streets. The lady explained she couldn't keep the dog because she had an apartment. Noah's Ark was full and simply couldn't take her. They told the woman she would have to take the dog to the city pound, which meant the dog would be done away with in three days if no one claimed her. Susan couldn't stand the thought of it, and made a deal with the woman who agreed to run an ad to find the owner. Susan would keep the dog until the owner called. The woman ran the ad and the owner called, but didn't want the dog because "It ran away all the time," he said.

We were growing attached to this gentle animal, which didn't bark, was easily cowed, and was always by our side. Susan was glad because she didn't want to let her go anyway, this dog we already had named Chelsea, this non-barking, tail-wagging dog. So Chelsea became a member of our household.

It was obvious Chelsea had been abused. She was afraid of everything and wouldn't bark for almost six months. It's no wonder she "ran away all the time." As the months and years went on, Chelsea seemed to want only to please us, to say hello to everyone she met, to be a vessel of love. The only thing she wouldn't do is voluntarily get wet. She'd jump over mud puddles to avoid water.

Many years later, when Chelsea was a regular, barking-dog member of our household, she and I took a trip to Northern Wisconsin. Susan couldn't join us. There was a spot in Wisconsin, about two hours from us, that had the best brownies in the State — delicious, thick, chocolate frosting brownies. I eagerly drove without a break, got gas, bought two brownies, ate one quickly to get my chocolate fix, then left the other one in the bag and put it on the dash of our truck while I went to browse through an antique store.

As I approached the truck after shopping, I remembered the brownie in the bag on the dash board. It wasn't there. I opened the passenger side door and saw the torn brownie bag on the floor. Chelsea looked at me, brownie crumbs in her whiskers. "You pig," I yelled. Chelsea now retreated to the window on the driver's side where she tried to disappear into the seat. "You ate my brownie!" I went on. "Then you tried to lie about it!" I stopped. I was beginning to sound like Gram.

Poor Chelsea already felt rotten. She didn't need me calling her a pig, and now a liar. But I couldn't help it, I had to get in one more yell. "You Pig!" I said again as I got into the truck. Then my anger left and I felt silly and rotten myself. Chelsea was slumped against the far window, her face away from me. I said, "Come here" in a gentle voice. That's all it took for Chelsea to forgive me, not only for my name calling and yelling, but for any and all injustices I or anyone else may have done to her. It was total absolution, total love, as she nuzzled me and lay with her head on my lap the rest of the trip.

Now, if that had been Mickey it would have been a different story. Mickey would have eaten the brownie and the bag. He wouldn't have left any crumbs, wouldn't have acted guilty, and would have taken my hand off if I dared slap him, and at least snarled if I yelled like that.

It seems like, maybe, there's a time for everything. When you're young, growing up with a bully uncle, and trying to develop a nasty disposition for your Golden Glove fights, get a vicious dog like Mickey. When you're older, starting to mellow, and happen to have an addiction to chocolate brownies, get a dog like Chelsea. She'll not only teach you a few lessons about life, she'll keep you from gaining weight, and won't bite your hand off in the process.

She Wasn't So Bad After All

"I don't know how old the dog was at the time, but I was about 43, old enough to have controlled my temper a little better than that. And the dog must have been around two or three, old enough not to have messed on the floor, especially right under the thermostat."

She Wasn't So Bad After All

Not all of my experiences with family dogs have been as positive as the ones with Chelsea and, more recently, Cozette. Before them, there was Coconut, a pedigreed West Highland Terrier. That's the white "Scotty" on the Black and White Scotch bottle.

I had never wanted a pedigree because of the expense. But when we got her, it had been a moment of weakness. My weakness. I had given my son, Mike, $25 to get a family dog when Mike was 12 years old. I thought we would have a nice mutt and he would have money left over, which I was going to be generous about and let him keep.

He had been gone about an hour when he called. I answered. "Hi, Mike. Did you get a dog?"

"Yeah, I found one. Is Mom there?"

"Yeah, I think she's upstairs. What kind of dog did you get?"

"It's a white dog. Is Mom there?"

"Well how much is it?"

"Can I talk to Mom?" I knew something was up, but I didn't quite know what. He talked to his mother, and we ended up with a dog that cost not $25, but $125. I wasn't to know that for a couple weeks, but I ended up paying for it. It was to be the first time Coconut got the best of me, but it wouldn't be the last. It even went on after the divorce, because I ended up with Coconut.

She had a way of making piles somewhere in the house, at the most unusual times, long after she had been house trained, and I always, always found it by stepping in it — sometimes in my bare feet in the dead of the night, where it squished between my toes, and sometimes in broad daylight in my bare feet, where it squished be-tween my toes, or worse, with my socks on, and once in a while with my shoes on, but always unexpectedly.

I once got up in the dead of night to turn up the thermostat and, in the darkness, stepped into one of her piles. "Ishy, squishy ...!" I screamed. "I stepped in her ishy, squishy ...!" I don't know how old the dog was at the time, but I was about 43, old enough to have con-trolled my temper a little better than that. And the dog must have been two or three, old enough not to have messed on the floor, especially right under the thermo-stat. I woke Susan up from a sound sleep because I couldn't think of anything else to say and kept repeating over and over, "I stepped in her ishy, squishy ...!" I was frozen now, nearly nude, under the thermostat, afraid to spread this stuff all over the carpet, and I needed help, first to get me out of there and, second, so I wouldn't kill her. Coconut I mean, not Susan.

Another time, we had dinner with a new couple we wanted to get to know better. It was our first social event with them. We suggested they stop over after dinner for some cards and, as we entered the front door, Coconut was standing there looking at me. I said, "Sue, look at Coconut. It's like she's inviting us in. Isn't that cute?" Then I realized it was most unusual for her to be just standing there, not sniffing or making a fuss over us or the new people, so I directed the rest of my conversation directly to Coconut. I said, "Did you do something? No, she couldn't have done anything. No. Did you do something, Coconut? No, no, no, she couldn't have done anything. Wait a minute, why are you standing there like that? I'll bet she did something? Did you do anything? I gotta look. I'm suspicious."

Our guests were taking their coats off and I was now racing through the house to see if Coconut had done anything. I stepped in it, this time with my shoes on, and I yelled, "You pig. You pig. She made a pile and I stepped in it! You pig! You lied to me didn't you? You pig!" I was stuck on this phrasing and kept repeating it in a very loud voice because I wanted her, Coconut, to hear me and she was not upstairs near me. She was downstairs, near Susan. So she won again, and made a fool of me in front of my new friends, who wouldn't let me forget the thing about calling her a pig, and the whole conversation with Coconut, and being so upset because she lied to me. "You pig" became our motto and byword with that couple and was put on a birthday cake which they bought for me in December of that year.

Susan and I later took Coconut with us on a trip to Superior Quetico National Forest. We paused in a walk through the forest and, when we started walking again, I stepped in one of Coconut's piles. She was older now and I knew it was her pile, not a wolf's pile or a bear's or a beaver's or something else's. It was hers. I knew because I had been stepping in those things for years and would know them anywhere. I was quite proud of myself because I didn't scream or swear or anything. It was as if Coconut had taken some sort of geometry or trigonometry and statistics or some such thing which allowed her to figure out trajectories and the odds of my walking in that exact place where she had just gone. I felt this in my bones, because it happened so many, many times in my yard. In fairness to her, and now that she's dead and buried, I've got to be fair to her, she did it in the yard much more than she did it in the house. But I would always step in it shortly after she did it. I can't recall ever stepping on a real dry, hard pile. I knew if I did, it wouldn't be hers.

After 14 years of this, to the day, she died quietly. And I felt very bad for both her and Susan, who loved her so much. So I agreed to bury Coconut in our back yard. Susan wrapped the dog in her favorite blanket and put her in a box with her rubber bone and a couple of other toys, and then put a rosary around her neck and cried a lot. She then showed me exactly where to bury her, under a walnut tree near the barn.

I felt very bad about her death and dug and dug through rocks and buried concrete and finally after a couple of hours of digging a relatively small hole, because she was a small dog, I was cursing her again, under my breath, of course, because every so often Susan would look out the window and I could see how bad she felt. I couldn't yell or scream or complain or even frown — and I realized Coconut had won again. We found a piece of marble behind the barn, and that became the headstone. Susan planted petunias over the grave and they bloomed all summer, and every so often I would look over there and think to myself, "Yeah, she wasn't so bad after all."

"A Single Leaf Falling"

Susan and I were getting ready to leave our Cherry Valley, Illinois, farm home in a couple of weeks to drive to Boulder, Colorado, and sign papers for a new house. We didn't know anyone out there, but a neighbor said what we hoped would be true, "You've got friends in Boulder. You just haven't met them yet."

I sat in the autumn coolness on the deck chair, thinking about our move, thinking of all that had gone before. I was watching a speck in the sky, keeping it in sight as I reached for my glasses near the coffee cup. Then I could see it clearly, a hawk, wings motionless, floating on a west wind until it moved beyond the roof, beyond sight.

Far above the spot where the hawk first appeared, another speck appeared, moving in the same direction, straight and fast, leaving a jet trail until it, too, disappeared beyond the roof. Then something else in motion caught my eye. I first thought it was a butterfly, but it was a whirlypod falling from a tree. A moth darted past the whirlypod as if dodging a fly swatter, and then it, too, disappeared.

I settled back, glasses off, coffee cup in hand, wishing for a moment, a kid's wish I know, but wishing it were summer still with butterflies again. I should be done daydreaming. I know that, but it's like those times on the flat rock early in the morning at Gram's house, drifting in memory. I still enjoy it, especially when I should be working.

The drifting takes me to last night. Susan was on the swing near the Gazebo. I sat near her and we talked, with the crickets singing and the moon so bright we thought our barn lights were on. We talked of our mosquito patrol, the swallows that swoop over our house and barn every evening and allow us this chance to enjoy the night. One of our dogs, Chelsea, sat by Susan's side. For a moment, time stood still on a cricket's chirp and a single leaf falling through the moonlight.

So there I sat on my deck chair in the autumn, wondering why moments like that don't happen more often, wondering what it is that makes "living in the moment" so difficult, so rare. Could I change and train myself so it could happen once a week or maybe even, and I hardly dare to say it, once a day?

My daydream was shattered as I caught sight of my pants belt, old and cracked. I haven't bought a new one in years because there are several new ones in the drawer, all too small. Someday I'll get to use those newer, smaller belts, I vow. But for now, I'll forget the hawk flying and the moonlit barn and the cricket's chirp and that single leaf falling. I've got a yard full of leaves to pick up and storm windows waiting in the barn.

Getting Back in Shape

When I was 40 years old, I read an article about a man 56 years old who ran up the walls of the Grand Canyon for exercise. In those days, I was jogging a mile a day on flat ground and feeling pretty good about myself. I thought, "I'm going to be like that guy if and when I ever get to be 56. I'll be running up and down the walls of the Grand Canyon and getting my picture in the papers because people will have forgotten someone had done it 16 years earlier. It'll be news again, and I'll be famous. I'll feel good being in such great shape and I'll be bragging like the guy in the picture about being in better shape than most professional athletes."

I was truly inspired. The clipping became part of my wallet, and once in a while I'd take it out, uncrinkle it, and tape it to the door of the refrigerator. When I was 42, I still had the article on my refrigerator, but I felt so good I stopped running. At 50, I thought, "Okay, so I'm not running, but I've got six years until my 56th birthday. Plenty of time." At 53, even though I had lost the clipping about that braggart, I thought, "Back in my college days, it never took me long to get in shape, just a few weeks of hard work. I'll start soon and, before you know it, I'll be running up and down the walls of the Grand Canyon like that jerk who got all the publicity so many years ago."

And then it happened. Many pounds heavier and not having run for the past several years, I passed 56. It was too late. I was depressed.

But it was not too late! Years earlier I had read an article about a man who, on his 75th birthday had run 75 miles. I had also saved that article, but kept it hidden in my "get in shape" file. I was going to pull it out after running up the walls of the Grand Canyon.

I'm inspired again. I'm going to run 75 miles when I'm 75. I'll still have time to get my picture in the magazine, because people will have forgotten about that old braggart. So the wheel turns, as the saying goes, and everything seems to work out.

A Heart Attack

"It all started to sound pretty silly as I tried to explain. I felt as if he was getting me into deep water, the way Gram used to when she kept asking questions."

A Heart Attack

I finally began to realize I'm getting older the day I went to the emergency room with what I thought was a heart attack. I was given an EKG test plus several others, then the doctor came in.

"So, how did this happen?"

"Well, I was boxing yesterday ...."

"You mean, 'boxing,' with gloves on?"

"I was sparring with this young guy trying to show him some things."

"Sparring? How does that differ from boxing?"

"We're not supposed to hit each other real hard. It's like a training session."

"Training? For whom?"

"For the young guy. I'm too old to be learning much more about boxing."

"I'm glad to hear you say that. Let's see you're ..." and he looks at my chart and calculates my age from the dates, ". . . 65?"

"Yeah. Well, I used to be a pretty good boxer and

didn't get hit often ...." and it all started to sound pretty silly as I tried to explain what happened. I felt as if he was getting me into deep water, the way Gram used to when she kept asking questions.

I could have told him I was wearing an upper body chest protector and a helmet, plus 16 ounce gloves, and looked like a character in a cheap science fiction movie, but I didn't. I figured he had heard enough of my explanations. And he did have other patients in the emergency room, some probably with real problems.

"Your heart's strong, but you apparently damaged the cartilage in your chest. It doesn't show up on x-rays," he said.

"So I don't have a heart problem?"

"No, your heart's fine, but I'd suggest you retire from sparring. You can work out, but don't get hit anymore." He smiled.

"What a nice doctor," I thought, "an actual human being." I said, "Yeah, I think you're right. Thanks a lot." I breathed a deep sigh of relief as he closed the door, then my chest hurt again. I wondered if he really knew what he was talking about.

Later, Tom told me I shouldn't be worrying anyway. Strong hearts are a family trait, he said. "We all die of alcoholism before our hearts give out. In fact," he said, "when we die, the authorities have to drive a stake through our hearts to stop them from beating."

The Fight Crowd

"Scott and I coughed heavily as we made it into the fresh night air. The smoke didn't seem to bother Billy. Two nights later, Susan and I heard Mahler's First Symphony at Macky Auditorium on the University of Colorado Campus."

The Fight Crowd

Buck and Tommy, two fighters from The Front Range Gym in Boulder, were having their first professional fights in Denver and everyone at The Front Range, including owner Dave Gaudette, were going. I wasn't planning to go, but anticipation kept building. Then Scott, another gym member who brought his 13-year-old son Billy to the gym, said he'd drive. So I decided to go with them.

Scott's wife had no intention of going. In fact, she really didn't want her son Billy to box at all. My wife Susan said the only way she would go would be if I knocked her out and took her there in a straight jacket. So Scott, Billy, and I went to add to the cheering section from the gym. As we drove in, Scott, a gentle sort, said, "Now Billy, if the girl carrying the sign telling which round it is exposes her breasts again, I want you to close your eyes." Billy said, "Sure, Dad."

We were early, so we ate at the Sports Bar downstairs in the fight arena. The bar was filled with smoke, and much of it drifted up to the arena where the noisy crowd was milling around looking for seats, drinking beer, smoking, feeling tough. Then it started, forty minutes late. A ring announcer came in, dressed in a tux, just like the ones in Las Vegas. The four ring girls, poised in their tights and skimpy blouses, were on the edge of the ring. The Bouncers walked around in their T-Shirts, showing tattoos and bulging muscles, hoping a riot would start.

A young, husky, tough-looking young woman came in to sing the National Anthem. Scott and I were choking in the smoke. The announcer, in an over excited voice, introduced the woman, who turned out to be the worst singer any of us had ever heard. Every time her voice cracked, the crowd hooted. Then she would stop, draw a breath, throw her hair back with one hand, threaten the audience with the other, and sing louder. At the end, she gave an inappropriate vibrato and the crowd jeered and whooped it up one more time. She didn't threaten the crowd this time, obviously thinking they loved it, and she finished with bows all around, like a matador who had just killed the bull.

The ring announcer introduced local fighters as the four girls, now in the center of the ring, threw out hats, T-shirts, and miniature boxing gloves to customers, who were reaching, spilling their beer, knocking over seats. A message flashed on four big screens blinking the names, nicknames, weights, and records of the fighters for the first bout. The screen competed with the announcer who was saying the same thing, while the ring girl carrying the "ROUND 1" sign pranced around the ring. The obvious fact that it had to be the first round since no one fought yet didn't seem to bother the girl or the audience.

As an ex-boxer, I was curious if not excited. Buck had 50 amateur fights, but hadn't fought in 20 years. He was fighting a world champion "kick-boxer" turned "boxer" who was short, tough, and impossible to knock out. Tony, Buck's trainer, an ex-fighter who was good enough as a pro to fight for the welterweight championship, told Buck, "Jab, move, stay away, score points. Don't try to knock him out." Not only did Buck ignore the advice, he threw away a round of energy dancing around the ring before the bell. His opponent stoically watched the dance. Buck should have saved it because he soon ran out of gas and his short, tough opponent almost killed him before Tony threw in the towel.

After the first fight I went to the bathroom. An older man was issuing towels for tips. Just like at the Waldorf. Except some customers took the towels, thinking it was another give-away. A few frills had changed since my fighting days at the Shrine Auditorium in Duluth. They now had ring girls, an announcer in a tux, big TV screens, and a man passing out towels in the washroom. But the basics hadn't changed. Smoke, noise, and a crowd feeling tough. It wasn't quite the thick blue haze of smoke that used to rise from the fight crowd at the Shrine Auditorium and hang under the ring lights where we had to fight, but there was plenty of smoke — and noise, louder now because of all the electronic gear.

It was getting late and the bouncers were more evident again, roaming the aisles, hoping it wasn't too late for a riot. But it was an orderly chaos with one final announcement before the crowd drove home. "Drink up, two drinks for the price of one." Everyone was leaving, pumped up and tough. They could have beaten those bums in the ring. Hell, they could even take on the flashy bouncers, but not tonight. The "old lady" would be waiting. Maybe next time. Scott and I coughed heavily as we made it into the fresh night air. The smoke didn't seem to bother Billy.

Two nights later, Susan and I heard Mahler's First Symphony at Macky Auditorium on the University of Colorado Campus. It was terrific, but it wasn't long before the older man in front of us was sound asleep. I looked at the 100 or so members of the Symphony and thought that none of them could go four rounds. But I also remembered the fights and didn't think any of the boxers I saw could play a violin.

I went to the men's room during intermission. There on the wall above the urinal, written in pencil, was the note, "Stop rape. Take Salesmanship 201." It was the only writing in the bathroom. A little different from the men's room at the fights where the messages weren't as subtle and were scratched or carved into the walls and stall doors with a sharp instrument. And at the concert there was no smoking, no beer or liquor sales, only chocolate chip cookies for sale in the outer lobby during intermission, and you couldn't bring the cookies into the hall itself. No paper mugs of beer were passed down the row the way they were at the fights, no near riot, no bouncers, and no noise. Only the beautiful strains of Mahler's First Symphony and the gentle snoring of the man sitting just ahead of us.

The Old Man In The Neighborhood

Susan and I used to wave to a neighbor, an old man, as we drove past his house. Once in a while he'd wave back. He wore sunglasses, moved slowly, and struck us as a grouchy old cuss. Two years of occasional waving as we drove by and occasional chitchat when we met him at the mailbox was the extent of our getting to know him.

One summer evening I met him along the golf course path where I was taking our dog Chelsea walking. The old man walked even slower than on his trips to the mailbox. Chelsea went up to him, tail wagging, sniffing an enthusiastic "hello."

"Oh hello there, old boy," he said as he slowly bent down to pet Chelsea. Chelsea was acting like this old guy was her long lost, best friend.

He straightened up and stuck out his hand to me. "I'm Bill," he said, "and your name?"

"Bob," I answered. "And this is Chelsea."

"It's a good name, Chelsea," he said, as he bent

over again to pet her. "How long you been in the neighborhood?" he asked.

"A couple of years." I said.

"I've been living here since 1965," he said. "Me and Angie."

"Then you're one of the original owners here, aren't you?"

"Me and Angie bought out here before most of these houses went up," he said, "but Angie died a month ago and it's not the same anymore."

I didn't expect that jolt. I wondered why we didn't know that and tried to recover. "I'm sorry to hear that. Susan, my wife's name is Susan, I know she'll be sorry too. We never met Angie," I said, feeling stupid at saying something so obvious. We hadn't even met Bill, not really. Chelsea already knew him better than I did. It was awkward now, but Chelsea provided my out. She saw a dog at the far end and pulled out of her collar. I hurriedly shook Bill's hand, pulled away, and said, "Good meeting you, Bill, but I gotta get her." and ran after Chelsea.

When I recovered Chelsea and was back in the house, I said to Susan, "You know the old guy in the sunglasses across the street? Well, I ran into him on the walkway and he and Chelsea really hit it off. We got talking and I found out his wife died a month ago. Her name was Angie."

"Oh, that's awful," Susan said, and then repeated what I said to Bill, "We never even met her."

A few months later Susan held a neighborhood Christmas party and invited Bill. He was a charming old guy, quiet, and friendly to everyone, especially Chelsea, who along with Cozette, was in the basement for the duration of the party, but let out briefly at Bill's request. They greeted each other again like old friends and then we had to put both dogs back in the basement until the party was over.

I walked Bill out the door and to the street so he wouldn't slip on the sidewalk. "You don't have to worry about me," he said. "I've reached the stage where I'm dispensable."

"Oh, that's not true, Bill," I said, holding his arm to support him, but again feeling awkward at suddenly knowing more than I was prepared for. "You can't say that," he admonished, startling me. And then in a quieter voice he said, "No, you're not me. You don't know how I feel, so you can't say that. I know the time's coming when the Guy," and he nodded to the sky, "He'll be calling me, and that's good." It was cold out and I only had a sweater on. I wanted to get back to the other guests and I wasn't sure what to say. So I asked what later struck me as a dumb question. "How old are you, Bill?" as if his answer would maybe justify his statement about being ready to die.

"I'm 85," he said.

"Wow, you don't look that old at all. Are you okay now?" I asked as we reached the street and he seemed ready to walk home.

"I'm fine," he said. "It was a nice party. Be sure to tell Susan."

"I will. Goodnight, Bill," I said, and I hurried to get back inside.

"Did you realize Bill was 85?" I asked Susan as we cleaned up after the party. "No kidding!" Susan said, and we didn't think much more about it. I didn't mention about him telling me he was ready to die. I didn't forget about it, but I just didn't want to talk about it.

A week later, I met Bill at the mailbox. "I want you and Susan to come over," he said.

"Sure, when do you ...?"

"Tonight." he said.

"I'll ask Susan and get back to you." I said.

Susan called and arranged for us to come over before 6 p.m. I rang the doorbell. He apparently didn't see Susan when he opened the door and said, "Where's your better half?"

"She's right here."

"Good," he said, and handed Susan a gift. He told her again what a nice party it was. She set the gift aside after thanking him and we went into his living room. A single play old phonograph, the kind I hadn't seen in many years, was playing Lawrence Welk on a vinyl, long play record. The wall opposite the phonograph was a ceiling to floor bookshelf completely filled with books. Books on Colorado filled an entire section and an ornately bound set of "Great Books of the Western World" was at eye level. "Angie read every one of them," he said. And then he showed us bound copies of the genealogy books Angie had done on both of their families. "She was the scholar in the family," he said.

Bill took us on a tour of the room and showed us pictures of himself and Angie on a mountain top with one of their children and another photo of them together in Hawaii. There was a three by four foot hand made note on the wall that was her happy birthday card to him. Part of it said, "I'll always love you, even though you're an old fart," and he chuckled when he saw us reading it.

The thing he seemed most proud of was a mural Angie had embroidered that hung on the same wall as the "old fart" card. It had a schoolhouse and church and dates for their wedding and the birth dates of all their children. In large letters, taking up almost half the mural was the saying "Love conquers all."

"That was Angie's favorite saying," he said. "She really believed in that." He returned to the overstuffed chair and we sat on the couch. "I was in the Air Force stationed in Corpus Christi and I loved to play poker with the boys. One day a friend of mine said, 'I got a date Saturday. She has a friend. Want to go?'"

"Well, hell...a blind date? I didn't know if I wanted to give up poker for a blind date, but I decided, okay, I'll go. Her name was Angie, he told me, and she lived with four other girls at this apartment off campus.

I was supposed to knock on the door at eight and introduce myself. He said Angie would answer the door." He smiled and became animated as he told us. "I knocked on the door and, you know, I couldn't believe it. Here was this beautiful redhead, and I said, 'Hi, I'm Bill. You must be Angie.' And she said, 'Hi, I'm Angie. You must be Bill.' Whenever we'd meet through the years after not seeing each other, I'd always say, 'Hi, I'm Bill. You must be Angie.' And she'd always say, 'Hi, I'm Angie. You must be Bill.' Yup," he said, "after I met Angie there was never any other woman for me."

Susan and I sat in silence on the couch. The record of Lawrence Welk had reached the end and the phonograph needle cycled in the return groove. Bill got up and put the arm back on its cradle. None of us spoke, and he came back to the chair. "We used to always call each other, 'Hon.' Never in front of anyone, only when we were alone. And that's the last word she spoke, 'Hon.'" He shrank into the chair and looked his age. Then he moved to the edge of the chair again and, wrestling with the thought, said, "So suddenly — that's what made it tough. Got lung cancer and died in 30 days."

What could we say? Susan spoke for both of us. "I wish we had met her, Bill."

"You'd have loved her," he said. With that he got up and showed us the hall closet where all her dresses hung. "She made her own dresses," he said and showed us the quality with his fingers.

After a long pause I remembered Susan had left supper on the stove. I told Bill we had to get going, but would visit again.

"You haven't opened the present yet," Bill said.

"Oh, can I open it now?" Susan asked.

"I'd like you to," he said.

She opened it, the present he obviously wrapped. It was a historical book on Colorado from his collection. He knew from a conversation with Susan at the party how much she enjoyed local history.

"Oh, Bill, it's a wonderful gift," Susan said, and hugged him.

"Angie and me were friends with the author. She signed it for us."

"I'll treasure it," she said. "Thank you so much."

"Wait for me, he said, and went into his bedroom. We were near the phonograph and the record was still spinning. Susan took the phonograph arm and put it at the beginning and Lawrence Welk started playing again as Bill walked out of the bedroom.

"I know you've got to go," he said. "Thanks for coming over." He escorted us to the door. "We enjoyed it, Bill. I'm glad we got to know you better," I said. He didn't say anything at first. Then he said, "It was a wonderful party, Susan. Angie would have really enjoyed it."

We walked into the cold air in silence. Bill died six months later.

Valentine's Day

Susan, Susan's mother Marie, and I were up before 7 a.m., and on our way for a Valentine's Day trip to Estes Park at 8:45. We drove past that small stone church on 63rd street, built in 1888, that always reminds us of an abandoned church and cemetery we came upon when we were lost on a Wisconsin back road one rainy Sunday so many years ago. Past Dakota Ranch, where a three year old boy was having a race with a chicken in the front yard, and the chicken was winning. Past horses and more horses and hay bales stacked and strewn near drinking ponds and rock piles. Past Elk Ranch and the small city of Hygiene where tuberculosis patients used to come to be cured in the days when dry air was the main treatment. Past The Trading Post and Stone Canyon Road into Lyons, elevation 5,374 feet.

We went past Horseshoe Bend Coffee House and Eagle Canyon to Huss Inn for brunch across from a 500 foot long rocky ridge called Steamboat Mountain. "In business since 1944," the menu said. We had traveled this way dozens of times, but this was the first time we noticed it. After brunch, we drove a Canyon Road that borders St. Vrain Creek, where its water flowed under the ice that stretched bank to bank and sometimes flowed in a narrow stream between the ice.

We stopped at Such A Deal Flea Market where Marie bought five paperback mysteries for $1.00 each and a phone for another dollar that she hoped would ring louder than the new one she just bought for $89.00. Susan and Marie tested the phone when we got home and it was louder. Such a deal.

That evening we ate Susan's delicious pesto shrimp and angel hair pasta and listened to Billie Holiday singing "Love Songs." We exchanged gifts. Susan bought Marie a Dr. Scholl's foot massager and Marie bought Susan a nifty, sexy lingerie piece. I had bought Valentine flowers the previous day. They sat in the middle of the table, next to four lit candles. It occurred to me I should have given Susan the sexy lingerie.

We went to bed early and watched TV and talked about Susan's planned trip to see her best friend, Letty, struggling with a life and death decision on Paul, her husband, totally paralyzed from a stroke a few days ago. He was thin, loved to work in his yard, was in apparent good health, but .... Letty, with the consent of the doctor and Paul's son, have agreed to remove all life support.

And Susan and I held each other tight.

A Trip Home Again

"The alley still crossed the lower part of this former yard of ours, the alley where we used to ride our bikes through a hail of BB gun fire, a part of our own training for the war that started on the day before my ninth birthday."

A Trip Home Again

I drove up Ninth Avenue West with Susan. It was the same steep, bumpy road that Tom and I used to walk to go to school, to St. Peter's Church on Sundays, and to the YMCA, where I learned to box, the sport that became my path out of this place so long ago. The wooden house with imitation brick siding, the chimney that was only half finished, the enclosed porch where the mailbox used to sit that Gram thought Big Helen always invaded to steal the mail, the back porch with boards missing, where Gram had to walk to feed the rabbits and chickens — it was all gone. The chicken coop, the old truck frame that was a makeshift saw mill, the small truck frame that was our neighborhood clubhouse, and the piles of lath and plaster that Tom and I used to break apart to use as kindling — all those were gone.

We could still see where the garden had been. The apple tree was still there, the one close to Fifth street, where the kids used to steal apples and Gram would put notes in the tree addressed "to all ye thieves," which never did any good. The alley still crossed the lower part of this former yard of ours, the alley where we used to ride our bikes through a hail of BB gun fire, a part of our own training for the war that started on the day before my ninth birthday. The grass that was never mowed and served as feed for our rabbits still wasn't mowed. We used to hide down in the grass as the bus went by hoping none of the girls from school would see us in our bib overalls picking grass. I'm surprised Tom and I didn't die of embarrassment before we ever got out of there.

That clunky house was gone, the house that kept us all together after Mom died, the house where winter winds rattled windows and blew fine snow through the bedroom window frame, snow that settled in small mounds on the heavy, always-padlocked metal trunk that sat under the window and provided us with our own indoor snowdrift through the coldest part of winter. That bedroom was so cold we dressed to go to bed. It was so cold our sisters' cheap perfume bottle froze and broke one winter and almost stunk Tom and me out of the room. That house had more scary hiding places than most haunted houses. It had an attic we weren't supposed to go in "because we might fall through the ceiling" — that was the official line, but the real reason was so we wouldn't rummage through the old papers and discover some family secrets. The attic and all the memories it held and secrets it hid were gone.

That mud-floored basement that had a coal bin at

one end and a fruit cellar at the other, that used to flood in the spring, when Benny, the lucky guy, got to paddle over to the fruit cellar in the galvanized tub and we wondered if we would ever get old enough to do that; that was gone, except for the outline. The kitchen cupboards that held Uncle Ned's glass eye and Gram's hoard of salts and home canned tomatoes, cupboards positioned over the trap door into the cellar, which was usually open and made us wonder why no one ever fell through it — those were gone.

Gram, who struggled so hard all her life to raise her own nine children, and then the five of us and a neighbor kid, and Chuckie and Lee Ann, Big Helen's kids for a few years, Gram, who never knew an easy life, whose husband ran away seven times and whose son, Uncle Ned, lived a drunken life in the same house, Gram was gone, too.

Uncle Ned, who terrorized us when we were small, before Benny came back from the Army and warned him not to touch us again, he was gone. His old and rusty Diamond T truck was gone, long ago towed away somewhere.

Mickey, our violent dog, too tough to get killed by the truck that almost ran over him and the car that sideswiped him, and by the chain that almost hanged him when he climbed the second story steps of Rigstad's grocery and fell through to the ground. Mickey was gone, ironically, laid to rest in peace.

I showed it to Susan as we drove up the hill. Now it was a piece of city property with long grass and the outline of what had been the basement, and the garden outline where the grass wasn't as tall. It was sold for taxes to help pay for Gram's hospitalization at the end, although Uncle Ned lived there for a few years after Gram died. It was a bittersweet place the long grass now hid, and the city would change further once it sold the lot to someone who would build a modern house in this now pretty nice neighborhood.

I never went back to look at the lot after that trip with Susan. Who wants to look at an empty lot? It held memories I'd have to dig up somewhere else. We always go through Duluth on our Canadian and Northern Minnesota fishing trips, but we make a wide berth around the lot that held the house on the corner of Ninth Avenue West and Fifth Street.

Camelot

"I don't want to think that far ahead or of all the possibilities. I just want to enjoy each day, drinking from that 'rare china cup.'"

Camelot

The climb that never ends, to a road that can't be moved, to a view I never thought could be mine — this must be Camelot, this city of Boulder, Colorado, a city I never heard of until Susan and I decided to move west in retirement.

So, I sit with Susan on a rock ledge at an elevation of about 6,000 feet, with our feet dangling over the edge, looking down at this beautiful city. Neither of us talk, but I'm thinking how lucky I feel and how happy I am to be married to Susan, to be healthy, to have good friends, a terrific brother, loving kids. Here we are, more than two decades later, a breast operation later, a hysterectomy later, many houses later, still together. And, if all goes well, we'll grow old together, me 110 and Susan 100, until one day we just disappear together. I don't want to think that far ahead or of all the possibilities. I just want to enjoy each day, drinking from that "rare china cup."

And I think back, beyond the view of Boulder, past the singing birds, through the crisp air, to twenty-plus years of alcoholism and the aberrant behavior that went with it, through a failed marriage, through financial bumps, to this rock overlooking "Camelot."

It has been a trip worth traveling, but, if I could do it again, knowing what I know now, I would have found this rock many, many years ago.

"And The Days Dwindle Down"

"A song haunts me each autumn — 'September Song.' It did when we first moved to Rockford and traveled to Wisconsin to watch the changing colors. It did in Cherry Valley when we'd sit in the Gazebo and watch the leaves fall around us, especially that night when the moon was so bright it lit up the inside of the barn."

"And The Days Dwindle Down"

Henry David Thoreau became my hero when I was about 33, guiding me to sleep on restless nights and helping me reach for, though I do not always find, simplicity. He was able to find beauty in a battle between red and black ants, in trying to determine the depth of Walden Pond, in studying a fence put up by a neighbor. So I've had years of reading and rereading Thoreau and of trying to see details and meaning in nature on solitary walks, especially on mountain trails in Colorado.

"There are three things important in life," he said, "simplicity, simplicity, simplicity." I seem to remember that only when I'm in the middle of some entanglement. Then I make lists of what to eliminate — and usually find myself adding to the lists as fast as I subtract from them. But mountain trails are invitations to simplicity. And I think I'm finally shedding complications faster than they grow back.

I know I'm on the right track. I have been ever since Benny took me to Swan Lake, three portages in from Brule Lake in the Boundary Waters of Minnesota. And since he led me in the woods to a deer stand in the November darkness to watch and hear the woods come alive with squirrels and ravens, and that first special time, to hear wolves howling, so far away I had to hold my breath not to drown them out. Today I'm most alive in woods or waters — always silent, solitary times.

A song haunts me each autumn — "September Song." It did when we first moved to Rockford and visited Wisconsin in the fall to watch the changing colors. It did in Cherry Valley when we'd sit in the Gazebo and watch the leaves fall around us, especially that night when the moon was so bright it lit up the inside of the barn. So many times, in walks with Susan, in times alone, I think of the words, "And the days dwindle down to a precious few ..."

At the end, Benny reminded me that time is short, that even a long life is a short journey, that we must live and love in each moment as deeply as we're capable of doing. One of the last things Benny said before he died was, "It all went so fast."

Tom, sent me an e-mail this morning: "Good morning, Bob. It's a beautiful day this a.m. I did my three miles and watched a fantastic sunrise. It got me reminiscing. I think the measuring stick for how well you've lived your life is how precious it becomes as you get older. Unhappy people endure their old age. People who have learned to live cherish each day."

Afterthoughts

An Unlikely Friendship,
An Enduring Inspiration

Meeting Louise Marston on that Saturday in September of 1950 had all the markings of a casual meeting like the thousands of casual meetings all of us have as we go through life. She was the Society Editor of The "Wisconsin State Journal." I was a 17-year-old coming to Madison to work on construction until I could get into the university. She spoke impeccable English. I used words like "ain't" and "he don't," sometimes in the same sentence, and I needed a tutor to pass freshman English. Her family could be traced to the Revolutionary War. Mine stopped with Grams' family in Wausau, Wisconsin, and with my dad's family in Seattle. She knew the governor, city officials and all the "important" people in Madison, and was perfectly at ease and in command of all social situations. She could not only introduce a roomful of people, she had an encyclopedic memory for dates and family history, and instant recall. I was shy around important people, and I thought most people who wore a tie and suit were important. She dressed in quality clothes and always looked as if she could attend the governor's reception. I dressed as if I were going to feed the chickens and rabbits with Gram. She was a world traveler, taking people on trips as a representative of AAA Travel, and then finding herself in great demand as a speaker describing her travels for the next several months for groups like Rotary, Kiwanis, and Executive Club luncheons. My trips were as a member of the Duluth Golden Gloves team to cities like St. Cloud and Hibbing, Minnesota, Sioux Falls, South Dakota, and Superior, Wisconsin, across the bay from Duluth. She never touched a drop of liquor in her life. I drank, a lot, until 1975.

She advised against my first marriage because I was too young and had two years of college left. I married anyway and divorced at 42. She never said, "I told you so." Two years after the divorce, I met Susan and we began to talk of marriage. I wanted Louise to meet Susan, so we arranged a dinner in Madison. After dinner and in front of Susan, Louise said, "Susan is one of the best things that has ever happened to you."

Louise introduced me to theater with her trip from Madison for an overnight stay at our home in Aurora, Illinois, and then a ride to Chicago to see "My Fair Lady" at the Schubert Theater. I introduced her to one of the wildest rides of her life when we started from home and reached the tollway only to realize I had forgotten the tickets, which were still on my night stand. I turned the car around, raced home for the tickets, then drove at breakneck speeds to Chicago. We arrived on time, but Louise never rode with me again without cautioning me to, "Be careful, young man. You may have Irish luck, but that doesn't make you immortal."

Our theater trips became an annual event as long as her health permitted, but one wild ride was enough. We would always meet in the lobby of The Palmer House before the theater, where she would stay the previous night after a day of Christmas shopping at Marshall Field. Then it was a leisurely walk to the theater.

She lived in the same building in Madison that she first moved into in 1934. I have moved at least 15 times since we met, and she claims to have a separate address book just to keep track of me. Since I moved to Boulder, a thousand miles from Madison, we have written weekly. We have dinner and visit at least once a year in Madison when I pass through on my way to Canada for fishing trips with my brother, Tom.

Louise has pernicious anemia, a condition that exhausts her if she does anything out of the ordinary. She has had a pacemaker for years and has survived a serious bout of cancer. She has always liked my telling her that, if she were a boxer, no one could have knocked her out, and that she's as tough as Gram was.

Ours has been an unlikely friendship and a blessing in my life. What is especially gratifying is that she tells me and others it has been a blessing in her life, too.

Since she entered my life on that fateful Saturday five decades ago, she has guided me with her wisdom and inspired me with her integrity, loyalty, and courage. I am grateful.